Allen & Elaine,

May your most precious
dreams come true,
What a great son you
have,

Peace,

Praise for Dan Pallotta and
When Your Moment Comes

"*Dan Pallotta is a hero in our modern age, and his book will change your life. It's not about achieving and forcing your way to the top; it's about rediscovering the imagination of a child and the powerful kindness of humanity.*

"*A dramatic departure from the 'self-help' books of the '90s, Dan's book will help you allow your deep-seated dreams to come to the surface in their own time. Stop listening to those voices who say 'you're not good enough' or 'that's impossible.' Dan's story will encourage you to begin living the dreams that have long lain dormant within you.*

"When Your Moment Comes *will inspire you to become a modern-day hero. Dan's writing has the conviction of John F. Kennedy and the compassion of Martin Luther King, Jr. His story will resonate in anyone who has ever dared to dream, and his book will alter your life—and the lives of countless others—forever.*"

— Sam Francis, publisher of *HERO* magazine

"*My husband told me for years that he wanted to be around when I finally found my place on earth and blossomed. Well, because of you (and these events), I am blooming in brilliant colors! I have not been directly affected by AIDS or breast cancer, but it doesn't matter. I can still make a difference. Thank you!*"

— Debbie Bennett

"*The souls you are touching by providing a container where people interact with people in a simple way of shared community . . . is life-changing in itself. Yes, we can change the world. One by one. Step by step!*"

— Eva Rose Goetz

"Because of the challenges you have allowed me to take, and the risks I have allowed myself to take, I am transforming my life—and it only took me 51 years! Thank you for your vision that has allowed so many to accomplish theirs."

— Connie Nicolai

"I simply want to tell you how profoundly you and your work has affected me. Keep up the great work. Keep up the good fight. You are making a huge difference in the world. And through you, I feel that I can be a very small part of it all."

— Russel Alan Davidson, Lt. Commander, U.S. Coast Guard

"You are a pioneer in encouraging humanity to emerge. Thank you for providing us with this opportunity to believe in others, and to believe in ourselves."

— Noni Karkos

WHEN
YOUR
MOMENT
COMES

WHEN YOUR MOMENT COMES

A Guide to Fulfilling Your Dreams
by a Man Who Has Led Thousands to Greatness

DAN PALLOTTA

JODERE
GROUP

Jodere Group, Inc.
San Diego, California

Published by: Jodere Group, Inc., P.O. Box 910147, San Diego, CA 92191-0147
(800) 569-1002 • www.jodere.com

Design: Paiwei Wei

"AIDSRide," "Pallotta TeamWorks," and "Breast Cancer 3-Day are registered trademarks of Pallotta TeamWorks. "Mobile City," "AIDS Vaccine Ride," and "I'mpossible" are service marks of Pallotta TeamWorks, pending federal registration.

Cataloging-in-Publication data available from the Library of Congress

Pallotta, Dan.
    When your moment comes : a guide to fulfilling your dreams by a man who has
    led thousands to greatness / Dan Pallotta.
        p. cm.
    ISBN 1-58872-007-1
    1. Self-actualization (Psychology) I. Title.

    BF637.S4 P33 2001
    158.1--dc21   20011029600

ISBN 1-58872-007-1

04 03 02 01   4 3 2 1
1st printing, June 2001

Printed in the United States of America

To my Mom and Dad, who gave me the foundation of love upon which I have built my life. To Kris, who helped me find a little child that got lost. To Alan, for showing me the simple power of kindness. And to everyone who has ever participated in, crewed in, donated to, or worked for a Pallotta TeamWorks event, for showing me that I am not alone in my dreams of a better world.

"There is a difference between one and another hour of life, in their authority and subsequent effect. Our faith comes in moments; our vice is habitual. Yet there is a depth in those brief moments which constrains us to ascribe more reality to them than to all other experiences."

Ralph Waldo Emerson

CONTENTS

Preface: Respectfully, What I Have to Offer   xiii

Introduction   1

Part I: The Foundation

Chapter 1: Human Beings Are Dreaming Creatures   11
Chapter 2: Letting Go of Your Fantasies   29
Chapter 3: Understanding Your Calling   45
Chapter 4: Allowing Your Dreams to Come to You   77

Part II: The Building

Chapter 5: The Trap of Cynicism   95
Chapter 6: The Awesome Power of Commitment   125
Chapter 7: Let the Obstacles Lead the Way   149
Chapter 8: Dealing with the Desire to Quit   159
Chapter 9: Moments to Come   175

Acknowledgments   185
About the Author   189

PREFACE

Respectfully, What I Have to Offer

Who am I, and what do I know about making dreams come true? Well, not everything, but I've made many of the things I've dreamed about a reality. Over the course of my 40 years, I've learned to fly an airplane; I was the second youngest person ever elected to the school board in my hometown of Melrose, Massachusetts; and in 1983, I motivated 40 of my Harvard classmates to join me on a 4,200-mile bike ride across America to help fight world hunger. I found an honest and soulful love in my life, and I've recorded and released an album of my own original music. But the achievement that probably lends the most credence to this book is Pallotta TeamWorks, which is the company that I started in 1992. My company has created a paradigm shift in the way that ordinary citizens are able to impact the great causes of the world. Pallotta TeamWorks, as of this writing, has raised more than $160 million net for the causes of AIDS and breast cancer.

In 1993, I had an idea: I had lost many friends to AIDS by this point, and I felt it was time for a bold response to the epidemic. It was time for a great journey—one that ordinary citizens could make, a journey of epic proportions that would serve as an appropriate metaphor for the journey our friends with AIDS were on.

The idea was called California AIDS Ride. It was to be a 500-mile bike ride from San Francisco to Los Angeles. We wanted 500 people to participate, and we hoped that by having each of them raise $2,000, we could raise $1 million for the cause. There were many who said it would never happen—that you could never get 500 non-athletic adults to bicycle 500 miles over the course of a week, and that even if you could, you'd never get each of them to raise $2,000. Well, we did—in fact, we did more than that. Each of our riders raised an average of $3,100, and we ended up grossing more than $1.6 million. We netted nearly as much as we had hoped to gross.

I knew then that we had struck a nerve with people. We had tapped in to their deep desire to make a serious impact in the world, and I knew that if this desire existed in California, it existed all over the nation and all over the world. The next year, California AIDS Ride tripled in size, and 1,800 riders raised an unheard-of gross sum of $5.5 million. We launched a three-day ride from Boston to New York. We had hoped it would gross $4.4 million. It grossed $7.4 million, and in its first year, became the single most successful AIDS fund-raiser in American history.

With the help of Tanqueray, our sponsor, we expanded the Rides to other parts of the nation. Then in 1998, we launched a new concept to help the fight against breast cancer. The idea was another long journey—a walk—but not your typical walk-a-thon. We created a bold, three-day, 60-mile journey from Santa Barbara all the way to Malibu. We hoped to net $2.5 million, but more than 2,000 people walked, and we netted an amazing $4.2 million in our first year—more than any of our events had ever netted in a single city. With the help of Avon, the sponsor of the "Breast Cancer 3-Days," as we call them, we went to Chicago, New York, and Atlanta in 1999. We raised more than $20 million for the cause in that year alone. So, in 2000 we expanded into Boston, Washington, and San Francisco. We netted more than $40 million for the cause in that year alone.

At the same time, we launched our first epic Alaska AIDS Vaccine Ride—500 miles over six days across Alaska—and netted $3.8 million for three of the world's leading AIDS research institutes. Based on the success of that event, we then added two new Vaccine Rides: one across Montana; and one from Montreal to Portland, Maine. So, eight years after this brave idea for a bike ride down the coast of California, Tanqueray's AIDSRides USA and the Avon Breast Cancer 3-Days have raised more money, more quickly, for AIDS and breast cancer charities than any known private event operation in history. In 1994, we raised a total of $1.6 million in gross donations. In 2001, we expect that number to grow to $135 million for the year, bringing our net total dollars

to charity close to a quarter of a *billion* dollars. We, and our participants, are now having more of a financial impact on the great issues of
social concern than many of the largest private foundations in America.

We have created a paradigm shift in two additional arenas. First,
we have brought for-profit business thinking to charitable fund-raising, employing the best practices in marketing, capitalization, man-
agement, and production. We believe that the realm of charitable
endeavor deserves nothing less than that. We believe that the great
causes of the world are not in competition with one another, but
rather, that together they are in competition with the great consumer
brands of the world—that they are in competition with everything else
that vies for the consumer's time, attention, and dollar; therefore, they
must employ the same intelligent, cutting-edge practices that the
Nikes, Apples, and BMWs of the world employ. Our strategy has
proven to be successful—in every city they have occurred in, our
events have broken virtually every record in the fund-raising books.

In addition, we stand for the proposition that you don't have to be
a martyr to make a difference in the world—that helping others need
not be a low-paying job. We believe that the brightest and most capable minds coming out of our best colleges and universities ought not
to be faced with a mutually exclusive choice between their security
interests and their altruism—between a good financial future and
making a difference in the world. We have created a business that
allows people to weave together their desire to do *well* and their desire
to do *good*, and we have stood on the forefront of the proposition that
it's time that such opportunities existed—that it's time to let go of a
quaint, small, and inadequate notion of charity; and create instead a
powerful, savvy, bold set of alternatives that attracts the best and the
brightest to the mission. It's time to bring the young Bill Gateses of the
world to the task of building powerful global institutions that address
the great issues of social concern *while* they're in their prime, not simply *after* they've made their fortunes.

Approximately 100,000 people have participated in one of our
life-changing bicycle or walking journeys, and more than three million Americans have donated to them. As the future unfolds, it is my
dream to enlarge our business to the point where one day, within my

lifetime, every American will be able to say that they've participated in or donated to one of our events and to have significantly impacted the way that Americans spend their discretionary time so that the pursuit of positive social change, through brave individual action based in kindness and compassion, becomes a natural part of every American's life.

Each of the accomplishments I've listed came to me originally as an *idea* when I wasn't looking and when I least expected it. I never forced them. Dreams begin with ideas. Ideas cannot be forced. Ideas come to us when they want to come to us, and not a moment before. I remember these macho gym teachers from high school who used to throw all these U.S. Marine Corps sayings at us. One of them had a really dangerous message: "Determination is the God within, and those who have it will surely win." Winning is their God. I don't think it should all be about winning. When you have winners, you have losers, and that's not very kind. *It's not about winning.*

So much of what is written about following your dreams is based on aggressive approaches—"Take control of your destiny," or "Become the driving force in your life," or other phrases based generally in the idea of forcing your dreams into reality. If you could control your destiny, it wouldn't be your destiny. I don't think God is crazy about people trying to control their destinies. Manifesting their destinies, yes, but controlling them, no. The approach must be more graceful than that. Let the ideas come to you in their own good time, just like television signals come to satellite dishes. You don't have to struggle to concoct the ideas. You want to be a receptor for the idea signals coming to you from out there in the great beyond. You want to be a receiver of your destiny. You have to have faith. You want to be aware when your moments come. You can't *make* them come—you can only be a good receptor. And then, after they've come to you, that's when you have to put in some good old-fashioned hard work.

Faith is about risk. Too many people want it to be without risk, and because it isn't, they choose not to believe. To have faith is to have courage. Faith means taking a risk that God really is there. There is a reward for that risk, eventually, and it's called *knowing.* Eventually, faith gives you evidence of the existence of a higher being. Without taking the risk, you can never get to the knowing, and you reinforce your disbelief. Risk is the currency of life, and, in the same vein, it's the ticket to meeting God.

This book is about being a good receptor, and it's about hard and smart work. It's about the idea that your moments *do* come, and it's about what to do when they arrive. It's also about making sure that you're not so busy with your own agenda that when your moments come . . . you end up missing them. But it's not about struggling to figure out your dreams or your destiny. It's not about coming up with the right scheme or strategy. It's certainly not about getting ahead. When you get ahead, someone gets left behind, by definition. To me, that's one of the biggest problems in the world. Maybe, if everyone stopped trying so hard to get ahead, no one would get left behind.

I think that our destinies are connected, and I think that part of what the "big satellite dish in the sky" is trying to tell us is that we need to make the world a better place for everyone to live in. That's not going to be accomplished by any of us getting ahead, so take the pressure off yourself. You don't need to worry that your life will pass you by. Stop being so hard on yourself. Ideas will not come to you when you're being unkind to yourself—and beating up on yourself because you aren't taking charge of your life is a very unkind thing to do. But in this age of the accomplishment rat race, that's what most of us are doing. Aren't you tired of that? We've confused things. *We've traded in the idea of a destiny for the idea of self-willed accomplishment. We measure everything in terms of money, instead of beauty, serenity, or fulfillment. We pressure ourselves to accomplish as much as the next person, and in that pressure, we're blocking the very ideas and impulses that lead us to our calling.*

On top of it, we're frightening that next person. Then they go out and buy some book about taking control of their destiny and getting ahead, which in turn frightens us even more, and then you have the vicious cycle of getting ahead that defines our modern world. No, this book is not about getting *ahead*. Sorry. This book is about getting *a heart*. This book is about a kinder approach.

This approach comes simply from the things I've learned about being a receptor for beautiful, magical ideas, and about manifesting them into reality. It comes from having the experience of my dreams coming true on a fairly regular basis. It's about what has worked for me. I don't claim to know how to make everyone's dreams come true, or even how to make *yours* come true. All I know is that I've done a few things in my own life that have worked. That's all I'm attempting to share. There's a saying I love that goes, "We teach what we most need to learn." To the degree that I'm teaching anything in this book, they are lessons of which I must continue to remind myself.

Throughout this book, you'll find questions in bold type. I invite you to reflect on them and think about them—try to do more than just breeze through them. It will double the value of the read. They'll help you make this your book, not just mine.

INTRODUCTION

In 1980, when I was 19 years old, I became the chairperson of the Harvard Hunger Action Committee. It was the undergraduate student committee at Harvard that was trying to raise awareness and money for the battle against hunger in the United States and around the world. The committee's largest effort was the organization of two fund-raisers every year to raise money for Oxfam America, an international hunger relief and development agency headquartered in Boston.

In 1980 and 1981, we organized two campus-wide fasts that each raised around $2,000 for Oxfam. It was a nice gesture, but I felt frustrated. I was involved with The Hunger Project at the time, and I was inspired and compelled by the statistics they were disseminating, which revealed that some 25 million people die of hunger and hunger-related diseases every year, and that two-thirds of these individuals are children. The Hunger Project had set a visionary goal in the 1980s of ending world hunger by the year 2000. The sheer boldness of it captured me. And the numbers kept me interested and impassioned: *40,000 people dying every day of hunger and hunger-related disease.* One particularly powerful piece of Hunger Project literature asked you to "imagine that you walked out to your doorstep and picked up the morning paper and the headline read: '40,000 People Died of Hunger Yesterday.' Then imagine that it said the same thing the next day and the next day and so on."

At the same time, I was taking some classes in development economics, and others on the world food system and trends in population growth. The disparities in life expectancy, infant mortality, and literacy rates between developed countries like the United States, and places like Bangladesh and Mali were sickening and sad to me. It was my first real exposure to just how many people were being left behind on humanity's

20th-century journey as some of us rush to get ahead, and my first real exposure to just how desperate being left behind looked. It looked like diphtheria, diarrhea, malaria, and starvation with no hospitals, no nurses, no food, and no roof over one's head. And it meant being one of a thousand faces in the same condition within a square mile. Horrible imagery. Horrible reality.

I felt that we weren't doing enough—not nearly enough. How could we stand by, knowing this was going on? If you saw someone run over by a car, and they were lying on the road, in pain, bleeding, and dying, you'd pull over to help. So why did we keep driving past sub-Saharan Africa? Why did we keep driving right by the starving children? Surely if there's a hell, it's reserved for the likes of us, I thought. I knew we had more potential than this. Much more. Our legacy, I felt, must be more inspiring. We were young. We were talented. We had the privilege of an education. We were at Harvard. People told us the world would be our oyster when we grew up. We should do more. This feeling grew in me, and it built into a great frustration because I didn't have an idea for what else we ought to do.

That changed on a bike ride one day near my parents' home in Massachusetts. An idea came to me—a big idea—to organize an epic bicycle journey across America the next summer, with dozens of students, all in the name of helping the hungry in the developing countries of the world. But it seemed like an impossible dream to me.

A few weeks later, school was back in session. I talked to my friend Mark Takano about the idea. We spent an afternoon writing down all the different things we'd have to think about. The next week, we began, just the two of us, to go around to the 13 different dining halls at Harvard with a little sign, a sign-up sheet, and some flyers, and we'd sit at a table at the entrance to the halls. When people would come in, we'd ask them, "Would you be interested in bicycling across America for hunger next summer?" The responses went something like this:

"No." "Yes." "No." "No." "No." "No." "Maybe." "No." "No." "No." "No." "No." "No." "No." "No." "No." "No."

A lot of people laughed at us. Some made fun of us. Every night we felt like quitting. But, largely as a result of our work in the Hunger Project, we had come to an understanding about what commitment is, and, rather than act out of what we *felt*, we were able to act out of our *commitment*, and we would stay at the table another half hour, another hour, and another half hour after that. But the feeling of wanting to quit was there every time someone laughed at us or rolled their eyes at us or made some kind of a joke, which was about every third person. And around 500 people came through every night. That's at least 100 bad jokes. That's a lot of feeling like quitting.

After a few weeks, we had about 3,000 people tell us, "no." That was the bad news. The good news was that we had about 60 yeses. Sixty may not sound like a lot, but you'd be surprised what you can get done with 60 people who have the fire of heroes inside of them—it's a lot more than what you can get done with 60 couch potatoes. So we had a big meeting for the people who said yes, and we explained the whole project to them. About 40 people ultimately ended up sticking with it.

We set up five different committees to share all the work that needed to be done: one for fund-raising, one for putting the route together, one for training, one for supplies, and one for media. The route committee gathered dozens and dozens of maps and pinpointed a basic rough route across the United States. They said we should take a northern route, because they had been told that bicycle tires tend to melt on the hot desert roads in the southern desert states. Whether it was true or not, it sure sounded harsh, and added to the epic sense of what we were doing. Then they went to every Kiwanis Club, church, synagogue, and Rotary Club directory they could find, and mailed about 2,000 personalized letters out to all these civic and religious groups, asking them three things: (1) Will you find a place for us to sleep for the night? (2) Will you feed us? and (3) Will you help us get local media coverage?

Well, it worked. Slowly but surely, these groups started to write back to us to offer shelter in function halls and gymnasiums, home-cooked meals and potluck dinners, and help with the media. As they wrote back, the route committee began to more specifically pinpoint where we'd be going, based on where there were promises of food, shelter, and showers. The other committees worked hard at all the things they had to do, too.

One woman on the supplies committee wrote a letter to the chairman of Ford Motor Company asking for a fully loaded custom van to go along with us. I thought she was shooting a little too high, but damned if the guy didn't write back and say yes to us, and we had this cool brand-new van with swivel captains' chairs and air conditioning. United Airlines paid for our plane tickets from Boston to Seattle, where the "Ride for Life," as it was called, was going to begin. U-Haul donated a big truck. We all went out and asked for pledges. We organized a giant cocktail hour to which we invited all of our professors, and then we asked them all to make pledges to us. The media committee got us commitments from lots of TV stations and from *The Today Show*. It was a grand effort—exactly what I'd been looking for. We were fully in the service of this dream, and as the year rolled on, the pace of our activity quickened and intensified, to the point that I really don't know how we had any time left for studying.

Ten months after the initial idea, we were ready to go. A few days after graduation (about 11 of us were seniors), 42 of us—39 riders and three support staff—went into Boston's Logan Airport with our duffel bags and boxed bikes, and we boarded a plane for Seattle. It was June of 1983.

Nine and a half weeks and 4,256 miles later, we arrived in Boston on our bikes. We had raised more than $80,000 for Oxfam (20 times what we were able to do with our little fund-raisers before), and had appeared on more than 50 local television news broadcasts. We got to ride around Shea Stadium before a Mets game to a standing ovation to the theme from *Chariots of Fire*—our images projected up on the Jumbo-Tron TV screen in the stands. We were interviewed by Bryant Gumbel on *The Today Show* and got to tell the entire nation about our story of commitment and accomplishment. Hundreds of wonderful people across the country baked casseroles for us, put us up in their high school gyms, made us pies, took us to McDonald's for breakfast, came out to cheer us on, took us in for home-cooked meals, put on banquets for us, shared their lives and their stories, and made us feel the true generosity of the American spirit.

It was magnificent. We had crossed Washington state; ridden past the breathtaking Cascades; across Oregon; across fields of mint in Idaho; through the rusty stone hues of Wyoming; up and up and up some more over the Rocky Mountains to a place in the Continental Divide called Togwotee Pass, which is a little over 9,000 feet. Twenty-six miles of downhill after we got to the top—nice reward. A few days after that, we could see the Rockies behind us. I can tell you that there's nothing quite like the feeling of looking back over your shoulder at the Rocky Mountains, knowing that you, your bicycle, your friends, and your dream have breached them. You get a particular sense of your potential knowing that you've climbed the Rockies.

We rode across big, flat Nebraska, measuring our progress by grain silos coming, passing, and . . . gone; across the beautiful rolling green hills of Iowa, Indiana, and Illinois; up and down and up and down and up and down again the rolling pain-in-the-ass Alleghenies in the draining Pennsylvania humidity; on to a meeting with the mayor of Washington, D.C.; past the White House and the Lincoln Memorial; up through Delaware, New Jersey, New York, Connecticut, Rhode Island, and then into Massachusetts, where we crested a hill that revealed the skyline of Boston—a view we had last seen from an airplane almost two and a half long months earlier. We had fulfilled, for that moment, our potential, and accomplished our dream. And I felt we had responded with everything we had to give to the dying children and adults of Africa, and to the cause of starvation everywhere.

Why have I told you this story? Because behind all of the magic and glory and the music that plays in one's head when you hear the telling of this story, there was always the desire to quit. And it was not insignificant. Each of us felt it. Almost constantly, we "felt" like quitting. Almost constantly, we didn't "feel" like doing it anymore. Not only during the riding, but during the organizing phase. It was tremendously demanding every step of the way.

Each time we heard a no from the people at the dining halls, Mark and I questioned why we were doing this. When we started mapping out the route and looked at how many meals and showers and shelters we would need—with less than eight months to get it done—it felt hopeless, and we felt like quitting. When we would go out for training rides in the cold of the Boston fall and winter, we felt particularly hopeless. We knew we were embarking on this 4,200-mile journey, but we had no time for serious training rides. On top of being full-time students, we all had committee assignments for the Ride that were keeping us extremely busy. Plus, most of us didn't even have bikes until later on in the year. So in the spring, we'd start to go out for these 25-mile rides, maybe 35-mile rides, and we were sore and exhausted when we were done, and realized we were not even close to being in shape for what was ahead of us. We were looking at 100-mile days on parts of the journey, and here we were getting in a 25-mile training ride once in a blue moon. That, in particular, made us feel like quitting.

Then, of course, there was the fighting. Forty college students, all frightened, all with their own ideas of how to best organize something, arguing for doing it *their* way. That was one of the worst parts of it. There were many times when it just felt so divisive that we'd never even make it to Seattle, let alone all the way back home to Boston on our bikes. And we felt like quitting.

And last, but not least, there was the ride itself. I remember the third day specifically. We were in Oregon, and I was incredibly sore from the 170 miles we'd just ridden over the last two days. We weren't even close to having begun, let alone close to being done. It was raining. We had a 75-mile stretch that day, it was morning, and we were only 20 miles into the day. I remember having a sort of panic attack. I remember saying, "I just can't do this. We're at mile 20. We have 20 miles to go to get to the lunch stop. I can't even go the next mile, let alone 20 to lunch. After that, there's another 35 miles to just get to the end of the day into camp. And that's not the end of the week. And even if we finish out the week, that's not the end of the month. We've got three more grueling weeks like this just to get to the end of the month. And that's not the end of the ride. We have another month and a half to go after that. I'm only 200 miles into this thing, and I've got 4,056 miles to go. I'm exhausted, sore, and wet, and I just want to go home. I want to go home real bad. And to get home, I need to do what I've just done over the last two days 20 more times. Twenty more times I have to go 200 miles. I can't even go another one, forget about 20 or 55 or 4,000. I want to quit, and I want to quit now."

In a moment like this, you're given the chance to create the person you want to be. A lot of people are out there looking to "find" themselves. I don't believe you "find" yourself. I believe that you *create* yourself. And the moment when the opportunity to create oneself is greatest is the moment that's the most difficult. And it can only be done by quieting the voices. By listening to what you're committed to instead of listening to what you're feeling. *What you're feeling doesn't matter. What you're committed to does.* If you can stay with your commitment—with your word—despite whatever horrible things you may be feeling or hearing inside your head, you can win the struggle. You can have your dream.

This boils down to a simple, sobering truth: *Achieving your dream is not easy.* It's hard work, plain and simple. Where most people get tripped up is in forgetting that. They forget how much hard work it is to achieve something truly remarkable, so when the going gets tough, they think something's wrong, and they quit. It's not because they're lazy. It's not because you're lazy. That is one of the myths we want to remove right now. *It is literally because you are not prepared, mentally and contextually.* You are not sufficiently absorbed in the fact that it will be hard work . . . to put the hard work into perspective while it's being done—to put the fear and the pain into perspective when it's happening. Anything that you don't expect is a surprise, right? When you get surprised, you often change course impulsively, without thought. With the proper context, the proper preparation, and the proper expectations, you can get through it. If you expect pain and fear and difficulty, then when it comes, you won't be surprised by it. You won't think something is wrong. And you will be less likely to quit.

The basis for what lies ahead is the notion that there is a basic set of principles that applies to dreams coming true, just as there are basic laws that apply to physics, chemistry, and mathematics. It's the ignorance of these laws that kills dreams. If you never studied mathematics, you'd never be able to solve a mathematics problem. If you don't understand the laws of dreams, at some level, you'll be much less adept at solving dream problems. Knowledge can make a difference. Making our dreams come true doesn't have to be a giant mystery.

PART I

THE FOUNDATION

Chapter One
Human Beings Are Dreaming Creatures

A Story about Dreaming

When Your Moment Comes is about having your dreams come true. Not *making* them come true, but *having* them come true. And not the dreams in your head, but the deep aspirations of your soul. The unrequited, unengaged quest to become the person you really are. It's not about goal-setting or creating strategies for measured achievement. It's about allowing the "you" that you always suspected existed to reveal itself continually. It's about the "you" unknown to you. It's not about getting a new home, a new car, or a new job. It's not about getting ahead. It's about a transformed way of being that is more authentic, more natural, less pressured, and more conducive to allowing the real you—the one you don't have to make any apologies for—to surface. We've been trained to be like everyone else. This is unnatural and fake. It leaves us always trying to measure up, and always falling short. Everyone else is *not* like you.

People whose dreams come true have given up completely on trying to "fit in." This book is about having that kind of courage—the courage to be a misfit. If you'll muster the courage to be a misfit—which is the very definition of faith—your dreams will begin to reveal themselves. And you'll fit in with the only person that matters—*you*. That's what this book is about. Unfortunately, this is not what most achievement books teach us. We've been conditioned to embrace a definition of life that is a mold—to be something other than our native, dreaming, odd, weird selves. We've been turned off to the idea of dreaming by a practical, cynical, homogenous, and cautious world lacking in courage and faith. This is about flying again—re-dreaming— and about discovering what that means for you, uniquely. Children know a dreamer when they see one. That's why I wanted to share with you this entry from my journal on the day I completed our 450-mile Alaska AIDS Vaccine Ride.

"I am writing this from the comfort of the Marriott hotel in Anchorage. In stark contrast to the comfort of this place lies all my gear from the last week, piled up in a corner—a wet towel with dry grass all over it, socks grungy with the dirt of the road, my helmet, a sleeping bag in need of airing out. Three pairs of drying cycling gloves. Surgical gloves I wore underneath all that in a vain attempt to keep my hands warm. And somewhere here in Anchorage, there are 1,497 other people sleeping late and ordering room service with the same array of sweaty, dirty, worn- out cycling gear lying on pretty hotel carpeting.

"My duffel bag is the very essence of a used-up Apollo com- mand module, and there were many times this week when we all felt like Apollo astronauts. We explored mountains that looked like the moon from the inside of our Gore-Tex jackets, hoods with hel- mets under them, bulky rain pants, and neoprene shoe coverings. The camelback water sacks we carried on our backs felt like smaller versions of the Apollo life-support backpacks.

"And we feel like we have just returned home from the moon. That elated sense of accomplishment that one can only feel when they throw themselves headlong into uncertainty, risk, and deep exploratory journeying into outer and inner worlds never before seen. It is the far reaches of human experience that fills each of us today. More than this sense of elation and

accomplishment human beings are not designed to feel. We have reached the limit of human experience for ourselves, at least in this moment. More than this we could not have given. More than this we could not process, at the level of the mind or the soul. Both are full, and both are empty.

"We spent a week inside an experience that felt as if it would never end. Each and every morning, I felt like quitting. There was a sense of dread in every day, as each of us counted down the number of days until it was over. But our experience was that it would never, ever end. And that made it all the more ominous. But now it has actually ended. Our minds were mistaken. Every single one of us made it, and we are all alive to tell about it. It's over. And people are signing up in droves to experience the dread all over again—some 300 or more people from the event have already signed up either to do it again, or to do the Montana Ride or the Canada-U.S. Ride next year.

"Tuesday was by far the toughest day. The toughest mental day of cycling in my entire life, including any of the days of my cross-country ride. Sixty-eight miles, all pretty much uphill, in temperatures in the 30s with rain and snow. After five miles, I began to lose feeling in my hands and feet. After ten, I could not feel them at all, and so we pedaled the rest of the way only being able to feel from our wrists and ankles up, not even being able to feel the shift or brake levers when we were moving them, but just looking down at the gears and the brakes—relying on eyesight instead of feeling to see if we had succeeded in adjusting them. 500 of us pedaled in to camp that day, and 1,000 were transported there. But every single person did their best—they went as far as their bodies and minds would take them.

"One evening, a man named Peter Sebanche spoke to us— he came all the way from Uganda to tell us about the reality of AIDS in his country, where dying AIDS victims lie on the dirty floors of the overcrowded hospitals because there are no beds, and there are no doctors to see them. Our suffering in the mountains seemed less against that image. He told us how his brother and his brother's wife both died of AIDS, and how he is caring for their four children, along with six of his own. In Uganda, nearly one in every ten people has AIDS. In Namibia, it is nearly one in every three. We were moved beyond words.

"There was a man I spoke with who was riding as his 60th birthday gift to himself; a mother whose 27-year-old son has AIDS. These people do not look like Greg LeMond [sic]. You can see their nonathletic-ness in how out of place their wrinkled faces and aging postures look in all the cycling gear. But they have the hearts of giants. Seeing senior citizens brave the same elements that bested some of the 30-year-olds is an inspiration not found in common experience. It really makes you ask the question, 'What is the limit of possibility?' Pondering the question alone seems to bring a kind of joy to my spirit—a great sense of excitement.

"There were brothers ands sisters riding together. Couples. Mothers. Fathers. We spoke to them about kindness and possibility and they were hungry for the message. Their souls were hungry for it.

"Yesterday, the last day, about five miles from camp, we went through a neighborhood of Native American people. Many small children came out to wave to us. In that place I came upon the most powerful sight I think I have ever seen. Five small children, ages four to eight, all about two or three feet tall—gathered around one of our D.C. riders, who is about six feet tall. In his red, white, black, and blue Spandex outfit, he looked very much like a superhero—the cycling outfits are not unlike the costumes of Superman and Superwoman. But it was more than the outfit that made him appear as Superman speaking to children. It was the way the children were rapt—looking at this larger-than-life figure who had just conquered their state, and who was speaking to them in a shimmering, futuristic helmet about children with AIDS, and about trying to find a cure for AIDS.

"Here was an adult who was telling them about dreaming—who was living his life to the fullest. Children nowadays are constantly surrounded by people and influences that limit them—that tell them to be practical, to put away their dreams, to get a *good-paying job. Here was this figure from another world come to tell them that it is okay to have your dreams—in fact, that dreams are wonderful, magical things that make life worth living, and that dreams, coupled with compassion, make superheroes, and that they can be superheroes too. You see, I think what draws kids to Superman is not just that he can fly, but that he uses his flying to conquer injustice, and to protect the weak and the abandoned. Very much what we all did this past week. We soared, in the name of justice and compassion. We became the superheroes of our own childhood fantasies in every way and at every level, and we are left with a powerful sense that we know not the limits of human possibility."*

I believe that human beings are dreaming creatures—that the imaginations we're endowed with as children are the essence of who we really are. We must dream and we must encourage ourselves to dream. I believe that when our ability to dream is suffocated or trampled on, when our imaginations are discouraged, when our ideas are ridiculed, when we are made to feel silly for dreaming—that is when our spirits die.

There's nothing I hate more than when someone says to me, "Now, you have to be practical about this." See, I don't believe that. There are plenty of people on the planet committed to being practical. Plenty of people holding on with a death grip to the status quo, under the illusion that there's some kind of security there. Plenty of people guarding the gates to change. The world doesn't need any more practical people. *Practical* is covered. The world needs more dreamers. The world needs more imagination. The world needs more ideas. More attempts at the *impossible*.

John Kennedy's famous words at Texas University ring permanently in my ears: "I believe that this nation should commit itself, before this decade is out, to the goal of landing a man on the moon and returning him safely to the earth." Where is the president who's saying we should go to Saturn? Where is the president who's saying that we should set, not a reasonable goal, but an *impossible* goal, to end the AIDS epidemic? These are the things for which we are hungry today—these and many others.

Everything that inspires us, everything that excites us, everything that makes us go "Wow!"—from the Empire State Building to those six spent Apollo lunar modules sitting on the surface of the moon this moment; from Disneyland to the four-minute mile; from the Emancipation Proclamation to a free South Africa—each one of these dreams was born out of some ridiculous, absurd human being with a dream.

My friend Herb says that the thing that distinguishes human beings from all other creatures on the planet is our ability to achieve the impossible. Gravity says that things fall, and human beings go buzzing around in these wild flying machines with engines, rotors, blades, and balloons in abject defiance of that. Elephants don't do that. Whales and dolphins don't do that. Physics says you can't travel faster than the speed of light, then a couple of human beings in a laboratory start experimenting with light and are actually able to bring it to a dead stop.

Our society, by and large, does not value dreaming. Our society values caution. Prudence. Reasonableness. Practicality. Our society does not value whimsy, risk-taking, or boldness. It values the status quo. It does not value change. Yet change, boldness, and risk-taking are the stuff that dreams are made of. It's essential, for anyone who wants to return to their dreams, to understand that we *are* dreaming creatures, but that we live in a society that attempts to tell us we're not. If you're not acutely aware of the fact that dreaming is in direct opposition to the world's system of inertia, then you'll think that you're doing something wrong, and you'll get discouraged. On the other hand, if you can contextualize yourself as a kind of superhero who's come to support a new, more vital and hopeful system, then your pursuit will be filled with a sense of mission that will bring you great joy. We are dreaming creatures. It's our job to help the world see that.

Children Are Dreaming Creatures

When I look back on my life, I see a lot of evidence of dreaming and imagining in my childhood, and I'll bet you can see it in your own as well. Imagination was everywhere. I spent my time constantly manifesting impossible little ideas that came to me. In fact, that initial sadness that comes to visit all of us at some point, came to me when the first adults started telling me I had to "grow up"—that I had to leave all these childish, impossible ideas behind, and become an adult and be reasonable and practical. Lucky for me, I said, "Screw that," and have gone on to extend my childhood now into my 40th year. But I almost succumbed to their pressure, and some of the more miserable years of my life were spent believing those so-called adults.

I grew up in Malden, Massachusetts—a working-class city of about 60,000 just north of Boston. My father was a construction worker, and my mother was a mom full-time. We lived in this two-family house, and it had a cellar like most houses in New England. It used to scare the bejesus out of me to be down there alone. My dad used to have a really cool workshop down there, with a big wooden table—almost looked like a kind of carpenter's altar piled up with all kinds of projects. On one end of the table was a big vise, and the surface was so covered with nuts and bolts and pieces of wood and metal that you couldn't even see the table itself. He was always inventing stuff down there. He was also always remodeling the house—he loved to tear down walls and open spaces up, which is actually an interesting metaphor. One of his projects was making a cedar closet for my mom, which took him about a month or two to build. When you build a cedar closet you get a lot of scraps of wood and stuff. At the time, I was about seven or eight years old, and I'd gather up all the scraps and see what I could make with them.

I decided I was going to build this spaceship, right down there in the cellar. I have this vivid recollection of a pink curtain my mom had thrown away that was going to be the hatch. I built a frame for it while my dad was sawing away at the cedar planks. And after I got it all put together, all I knew was that my spaceship needed a switch. You can't get anything to go unless you have a switch, right? You've got to be able to pull a switch, so the switch became very important. It wasn't connected to anything—I didn't know it had to be—I just knew you needed to have one. And I can remember going to bed being very excited about the switch going in. But the most salient piece of the whole story was this—not once did it cross my mind that this machine wouldn't fly. Not once. I just used to imagine flying around in space in this box with a curtain for a door—flying around in this impossible machine, and the thought *never* occurred to me that this would not happen. As a child, I was programmed for imagination—not for cynicism or impossibility. Every fiber in my being was excited about that damned thing flying.

I don't remember what I ended up doing when I pulled the switch and nothing happened. I probably started to pretend that I needed to do more work on the engine—the engine that didn't even exist—but you see, right there, it's the nature of children to work on engines that don't even exist. They just do impossible things, and they're convinced that it's all actually happening.

Do you recall your own childhood? Was there evidence of dreaming? What did you pretend to be back then? What did you play with? What were the things you made? Can you picture yourself making them? What do you feel about that child in the picture?

When we were children, my sister Nancy and I used to pal around together all the time—we were about a year apart. We were around five and six, and the kids in the house next door were the same ages as us. The four of us were always together for about four good years.

Bobby was taking trumpet lessons, Diane was learning the drums, Nancy was learning the accordion, and I was learning guitar. One day we decided to start a band. Now the funny thing about this band was that we didn't know that everyone in a band is supposed to play the same song at the same time. Each one of us was learning a different song from our teachers. I remember incessantly having to practice "Tom Dooley." We all got our instruments, lined up on the back porch, and me, being a type-A personality, just looked at everyone, and at some point said, "Go." And then we each went into our own little worlds and started playing four completely different songs, all together, all at the same time. We knew something was wrong, but we didn't know what, so we just kept playing. "The Impossible Band." Each member plays a different song at the same time. Now wouldn't it be great if the world worked that way? We were dreaming creatures, right from the start—Nancy, Bobby, Diane, and me.

Later that year, after The Impossible Band disbanded, my dad helped me build a go-kart. I could picture it entirely finished in my head. I used to dream about it when I went to sleep. I wanted it to be red—it's funny that red is the corporate color of Pallotta TeamWorks today. Red is the color of blood and passion and the heart. I love red. I was never allowed to use paint before, so it was really cool to think of being able to paint the go-kart. My mom was throwing away a gold vinyl shower curtain, so I gave the go-kart a few coats of paint—until it was solid red—and then I upholstered the seat with the gold shower curtain. Then I got some gold metallic trim paint, which was just dreamy—and that's exactly what I was doing while I was painting it—dreaming. Can a little kid have a car just like adults do, exactly the color he wants, with gold upholstery to boot? It's impossible. So what does a kid do? Defies that notion and builds his own, and it's impossible no more.

Teenagers Are Dreaming Creatures

When I was 15 years old, my parents took us to Disneyland as part of a two-week trip out west. This was pretty unheard of—California just wasn't someplace a working-class family from Boston went in the '70s. New Hampshire and Maine were the horizon, because that was all people could afford. But my parents saved up for this trip for us on a construction worker's salary. This was their dream—to show their children places they'd never gotten a chance to see themselves when they were kids. Big places. Big things. My mom and dad had dreamed of taking us to Disneyland for years, but never really believed they would actually get us there. We were all in Disneyland on the 4th of July in 1976.

I'll never forget the magic of that night. First of all, just being in the midst of Walt Disney's fantasy—one of the great dreams of the modern age—was powerful enough. But then there were the thousands of people gathered there that night. Perfect strangers in tears with one another, singing "God Bless America"—singing for the love of their country, and feeling undeniably connected to each other. For the first time, I had the feeling that this is the way the world ought to be—people should be singing with each other instead of fighting with one another. It's not enough to just not fight. We should be singing with each other. Impossible, right? But there it was, happening—for everyone to see—and it wasn't lost on me. I etched that image in my mind. It was a formative experience that has become one of the underlying principles and strengths of all of Pallotta TeamWorks' events. People cry together, struggle together, and they sing together.

But I remember leaving Disneyland—walking under those arches we had entered into three days earlier, with the monorail buzzing over our heads—and I never felt so sad in all my life. I didn't know if I'd ever be back in that magical, wonderful, utterly impossible place. My soul was sad, because for three days, it had returned home. "Home" was a place where dreams come true, where nothing is impossible, anything can happen, and there are no limits to how wild, fun, beautiful, and incredible life can get. You know, as adults—not human beings, but adults—we place limits on how beautiful things can be. On this deep blue marble with swirly white cotton clouds over green oases, with waterfalls and mountains twirling and hurdling at 15,000 miles an hour through the twinkly stars in the blackness of space—on this magical stage, we place limits on the potential of beauty. Let me share with you a quote that I love: "I have always envisioned a God that dances." When I first heard that, I said to myself, "Of course God would dance. God is the source of all beauty and joy. It's the source of rainbows, the toucan, the Alps, the tulip. Of course God would dance."

So, I was sad to leave Disneyland. Because Disneyland said that God dances, and that you can wish upon a star and your dream will come true—this resonated with me to my very essence—and I was leaving that place for the sorry, weary alternative that adults had created outside of its gates.

Do you remember something that you had to leave or that went away from you in your childhood that made you sad? What was it? Why were you sad? Did you ever see it again?

Well, I wasn't going to leave it at that. While I was at Disneyland, there were a lot of things that struck me. I loved the imagination of Main Street. I loved the giant *Mark Twain* Mississippi riverboat they had out on their man-made lake. So when we got back home later in July, the first thing I did was go to the hobby store. I bought a bunch of balsa wood, paints, and dowels—everything I would need to build a replica of the *Mark Twain*. I wasn't going to let go of Disneyland. No way.

I had a photograph of the *Mark Twain*, but it wasn't a great one, so mostly I had to re-create the boat in my mind. I used some plywood for the bottom, and then I built it up from there. And I built it all with tremendous attention to detail. I remembered the detail in Disneyland—a sign was never just a sign—it had four or five layers of molding, lights all over it, wooden garnishes and swirls, and many colors of paint. There was something about the flushing out of imagination to that level of detail that pays a particular kind of homage to dreaming. So I did the same with my boat. I called it the *Walt Disney*. It had hardwood floors, which I coated with six coats of shellac each to get them to shine. It had painted white railings around each deck, and they looked so pretty against the blonde of the hardwood floors. There were benches I built for imaginary people to sit on. There was a band organ—a red one, with aluminum cymbals and a keyboard and everything—called the "Sadie Mae." There was a refreshment stand, complete with signs that said how much the milkshakes were. There were curtains at the back of the refreshment stand, and there were images of Minnie and Mickey Mouse on the sides of the boat next to the windows with the curtains on the upper deck. And it really floated!

I still have the *Walt Disney*. I was very attached to it and protective of it throughout my life. After I moved away from home, my dad called me all throughout my 20s, saying he was cleaning up the attic and could he throw the goddamned thing out? I used to jokingly tell him that he better not or I'd never speak to him again. But to me, it was like some Army guy's picture of his sweetheart that he keeps in his wallet on his tour of duty—the one thing that gives him hope and strength. The *Walt Disney* was my link to the dreams of my childhood, and I had to protect it. This speaks, again, to dreams being a part of our very nature. A year ago, my dad boxed up the *Walt Disney* and mailed it to me in California. I have it up in a second office

I have here at our headquarters that also doubles as a model rocket shop—in fact, I'm building a four-foot-tall model rocket right now. The *Walt Disney* needs some refurbishing, but I look at it today and it reminds me of my childhood, and of the essence we all have inside.

What did you dream of as a teenager? What do you have around you today that reminds you of those days, or of your essence? If you don't have anything, why not, and is there a way you can re-create something from that time? What do you wish you had around you? What conversation would it stimulate? What would it tell you about yourself? What single thing from those years conjures up images of you as a creative, dreaming person? What did you dream of as a teenager?

When I went back to school in the fall, I was in the tenth grade. I walked by Ell Pond, as I had for years before. Ell Pond always smelled of dead fish. It was a beautiful pond, actually, right on the edge of Main Street at the end of the business district, and right across from the junior high and high schools. But there were dead fish along the edges and trash knocking up against the banks. And I started to imagine a different Ell Pond.

I started to think about paddleboats that people could rent and take out onto the water; about a bandstand that would play live music on Friday and Saturday nights; about a light show out on the pond; about a small riverboat that would go around, all lit up with little white lights at night; and about floating Christmas displays in the wintertime. I started to imagine this grand, cozy, beautiful, magical transformation of Ell Pond—a gem, right in the middle of our city.

I put this all in the form of a written plan and I called the mayor's office. Me—15 years old—asking for an appointment with the mayor. I actually got the appointment, and I went in there with my friend Bill Bailey, whom I had somehow convinced to be my partner in this, and, at the very least, make it look like I was proposing something that was generating popular support. So we went into the mayor's office and I made my presentation to the mayor himself—with drawings and all—and it couldn't have been met with a flatter response. The mayor had a dozen reasons why it wasn't practical, wasn't affordable, wouldn't work, and was otherwise not a good idea. I was totally depressed. That's what happens when the dreamer in you is not acknowledged or nurtured.

Can you think of things you've been excited about that someone discouraged? Do you remember how you felt when that happened? Did it stop you, or did you go forward? What does that tell you about yourself—about your soul? What decisions did you make after those kinds of occurrences?

We Are More Alive When We're Dreaming

Did you ever notice how people are more alive when they're pursuing a dream? They're ignited. Look at how inspired people get when they watch the Olympics. They love to watch dreamers. They love to watch people exploring the limits of their physicality and psychology. They invest a part of themselves in the Olga Korbuts, the Franz Klammers, Peggy Flemings, Muhammad Alis, and Greg Louganises. There is probably no group of people in the country more beloved than our Olympic athletes. Why? Because they aspire to run quicker, swim faster, jump farther, skate more gracefully, or ski more swiftly than any human being in all history—they explore the far outer reaches of human potential.

I remember a particular example from my childhood: My dad once said something that helped to reawaken the dreamer in me. I was a goalie on our hockey team, and we had a pretty bad team. We used to lose by football scores—18 to 1, 21 to 3—it was terrible. My dad used to take me out in the driveway and practice shooting tennis balls at me so I'd get better. Then one day he said to me, "If you're good enough, they'll give you the most valuable player trophy."

I was so depressed by how much we always lost, and I felt like I was such a terrible goalie, that his words didn't penetrate. I said, kind of depressed, "They don't give MVP trophies to goalies."

He said, "Well, hey, if you're good enough, they'll make a special trophy for you."

That sparked my imagination. That made me listen. There was vision in it. There was impossibility in it. It was a bold idea—a whole new trophy, just for me. Now that's something I could get excited about. After that, I got into practicing harder than I ever had before.

That next year, we won the championship in our league. I was ten years old, and at the big end-of-the-season dinner for all the teams, they were giving out trophies for the best players and the most improved players. There was a kid on our team named Patrick who we all wanted to win the MVP trophy instead of this other kid who was kind of a coach's favorite. So there we all were rooting for Patrick. They said they were about to announce the MVP, and we were sitting on the edge of our seats. We waited, and the name came over the speaker: "Danny Pallotta." Well, I couldn't believe it. It wasn't a special trophy just for goalies, but it was an impossible dream come true. My dad was protecting the dreamer in me.

My dad recently called me and said he wanted to do our Montana AIDS Vaccine Ride with me. It's an arduous, 500-mile, six-day ride up and over the Continental Divide—all the way from Missoula, Montana, to Billings. My father is not an athlete—he hasn't been on a bike in 40 years. In fact, he'll be 66 years old, and he has to go to the doctor to make sure he's okay to start a training program. He's going to train on a treadmill during the winter and then start riding in early spring. But it's yet another example of the dreamer in us. He's so turned on by the idea of doing this—at the age of 66—not because it's going to be fun, but because it's going to be difficult. There's a level at which the soul needs to be challenged, to be invited to do the impossible, and that's exactly what this feels like to him. When he called to give me the news, I heard an excitement in his voice that I really had never heard before.

I've seen people in their 70s and 80s riding in our 500-mile bike rides for AIDS and walking in our 60-mile 3-Days for breast cancer, and they're so much more alive than many 25-year-olds I know who have completely given up on themselves. Where there's a dream, there's life, and where there's none, there's only gray—and on a 25-year-old, gray doesn't look that good.

Last year, my mom, my two sisters, and I did the Breast Cancer 3-Day in Boston. We walked 60 miles, from Leominster all the way back to

Boston. On the second day, as we were walking into camp, my mom's mother, Hazel, was waiting there with my dad and some others, and when she saw my mom, she ran up to her, hugged her, and said, "Oh, Patsy, I'm so proud of you." I could see how much that meant to my mom, and it actually made me cry to see her getting that kind of acknowledgment from her own mother. And it happened because she was pursuing a dream. She was inspiring her own mother. There was life and vitality in that moment.

The next day, when we got into the closing-ceremony area, most of the walkers were already in. When we came in, everyone was all there waiting for the last walkers, and when they saw my mom, they let out this huge cheer. She's a 12-year breast cancer survivor, and they all knew her story because I had told it from the stage several times. There were tears in my mom's eyes as she walked in. She had never accomplished anything like this, and she had never been acknowledged by a cheering crowd as a returning hero. Her soul was finally expressing itself, and there was a joy in her face in that moment that I had never seen before. Not only are children and teenagers dreaming creatures, but our mother, fathers, and even grandparents are dreaming creatures, too. And they are more alive when they're expressing it.

Did your parents encourage the dreamer in you, or did they discourage it? How much has that influenced the path of your life? What patterns has this set for you as a dreamer—a risk taker? Was there anyone that encouraged the dreamer in you? Can you remember people from your childhood who rebelled against conformity—who went after their dreams? Who were they? What did you think of them? What talents did you exhibit as a child that you wish someone had been more supportive of?

There were lots of other examples of dreaming in my own childhood, which are too numerous to describe in detail—I built a space shuttle from scratch; a tennis ball thrower; a gigantic, clunky rolling refreshments cart that we used to sell Italian sausages out of down at Pine Banks baseball park; lots of model rockets; and tons of drawings, plans, and more. After I saw *Willie Wonka and the Chocolate Factory*, I began designing a house the size of a shopping mall—with roads coming off the main hallway, and little electric go-karts to transport the guests around. Strange how the visions of your childhood come back to you if you hold on to your dreams—Willie Wonka's factory kind of describes the new headquarters we're building for Pallotta TeamWorks, but with a healthy dose of humility in the interior design.

The dreamer continued expressing in me through my teenage years. I did well in school—pretty much an "A" student—and the future seemed limitless. I was the president of my high school class. I was on the debate team. I played goalie on my freshman and junior varsity hockey teams—along with at least one teammate who subsequently made it into the NHL. I had been accepted to three Ivy League colleges. But I wasn't aware of what was about to happen to me.

I can remember lying on my back in the pool in the summertime. I'd lay there and look up at the clouds, and I felt my whole future ahead of me. I could picture all kinds of faces and images in the clouds. I wanted to be president of the United States, and I was convinced I would be. I would run for the state senate, and serve there a few years. Then I would run for governor of Massachusetts, and serve a couple of terms there—then I would run for president. I wanted to be a young president, like Kennedy. And I wanted to change the world. There I was, 17 years old, floating in the pool, dreaming of being president of the United States, without one good reason why it wouldn't happen. I was connected with my essence.

Most of us, if we were lucky enough, have tons of evidence of the dreamer in us from our childhoods. I try to keep reminders of my childhood all around me. I have a teepee in my backyard, squirt guns and hockey sticks in my office, musical Winnie the Pooh and Mickey Mouse figures on my office bookshelf, stuffed animals, Slinkies, Silly Putty, baseball gloves, and footballs on my desk. My whole house is like a cowboy's place, with saddles, saloon mirrors, Indian drums, and ranch cowboy furniture. I always wanted to be a cowboy when I was a little kid. I used to dress up and pretend to be one then, like a lot of little kids. I'm still one now. There's not very much about me that's adult. I don't much care for adults. I don't want to be a "dult." No, that's not a typo. A "dult." Almost identical to "dull." Don't be a "dult." Be a dreamer. That's your heritage. It's what you were born to be. And don't you let anyone tell you otherwise.

Are you a "dult"? Would a child think you are? Why? Who are the people in your life who are? What makes them seem so to you? How would a child react to them? How would a child react to you? Would you encourage a child's dreaming? When do you first remember adults trying to pull you into the realm of practicality? Do you work for "dults"? Do you enjoy it? Who do you think is more naive, them or you? What brings out the child in you? Who did you pretend to be when you were a child? What did you pretend to do? When did you begin to ignore your dreamer? What is the dream you would like to reclaim? How can you start to do that now?

Chapter Two
Letting Go of
Your Fantasies

A Dark Song Near the End of a Dark Time

This is a song I wrote around 1991 that was recorded by Edgar Winter for a horror movie called *Netherworld*. The title of the movie was an eerie summary of my inner world at the time. This song is entitled "Stranger to Love." At the time, I was not only a stranger to love; I had become a stranger to myself—a stranger to that child who used to dream without limitation. When you become estranged from yourself, you become estranged from your dreams, too, and there is no way of reclaiming them without facing the real, hard issues in your life. It is in this setting that most people start chasing after their fantasies as a means of escape, and at the expense of their dreams. This song actually represented the beginning of a consciousness about just how far I had strayed from my self—my ideal. It was one of the first times I was able to actually describe the state I'd arrived at, and the state from which I was finally ready to depart.

Stranger to Love

Well I'm looking for a land called love in this sea
Water's all I ever see around me
The night gets black and the night gets deep
Mother of Jesus have mercy on me

Love is your ma and love is your dad
You grow up, now ain't that sad
Love is a house, a wife and kids
My Daddy had the courage
I never did

Love is a word in the dictionary
Words ain't real they're imaginary
People writin' songs and people writin' books
They got love on their lips like a fisherman's hook
I'm a stranger to love

Love is a country I've never been
Well I wonder if it's like the pictures I've seen
I had a girl made me crazy with fear
Heard she's getting married later this year
Love is a feather, pretty and soft
So how come it keeps scarin' me off?

They say it's real
But I always feel
Like I'm a stranger to love

Commitment is the road to freedom they say
Road I'm takin' goes the other way
Where it leads, God only knows
Look out Momma, here I go

I'm a stranger to love

This chapter is about getting real about your life—letting go of your fantasies, uncovering the things from which you might be hiding, and taking responsibility for them. Many of us confuse dreams with fantasies, but fantasy is often a means of avoiding responsibility and escaping the real issues in our lives. It's different from aspiration. Fantasy is of the mind. Aspiration is of the soul. Fantasies are schemes of our own self-will. Dreams come from the will of God. A lot of people, a lot of times, confuse fantasies with dreams, and then they wonder why they won't come true. They don't come true because they're not *meant* to come true. In fact, it would almost be worse for you if any of your schemes *did* come true. Schemes and strategies and fantasies *can* work, but just because they do, it doesn't mean they're why you're here. And they're certainly not going to bring you the kind of fulfillment you're looking for. Our souls are looking for the fulfillment that comes from a sense of purposeful destiny. A lot of times we get sucked into fantasies—both others and our own, because we are either out of touch with our calling, or we're out of touch with our lives.

You shouldn't start concocting dreams without a sense of your calling—that sense of what we're put on this planet to do. And you can't get in touch with your calling without being real about your life.

In the next chapter, I'll discuss how each of us has a calling that is uniquely our own. Your dreams flow out of your calling. To try to make a dream come true without a sense of your calling would be one of the more frustrating experiences of your life. It would have no context, no place. In addition, it would feel incredibly inauthentic—silly, even.

This chapter, however, is about taking responsibility for your life. You can't even begin to listen to your calling and follow your dreams until you're doing that.

Put Your Life Before Your Calling

For a few pages, I'm going to take you into a very personal part of my life—a period that exemplifies everything I'm talking about here.

There was a ten-year period in my life when my dreams simply wouldn't manifest. From about the age of 21 to around 31, hardly a single inspired thing occurred in my life. No ideas came to me. It was a very dark period—a time when I lost virtually all my self-respect and self-regard. I became completely separated from that little dreamer, the 17-year-old who aspired to be president of the United States. My behaviors became so self-destructive that I began to dislike, and then hate, myself. I was ashamed of myself and living a double life. I felt that the ideal I'd had of myself as a child and a teenager was lost to me forever, and that my life was going to be a waste.

At some point, around the age of 20, while I was a sophomore or junior in college, I began to feel that something was wrong. I was losing my focus. I wasn't zeroing in on my dreams. I wasn't headed for my potential. I was distracted. Other kids at Harvard were on a fast track to ambitious career goals—they wanted to be doctors, lawyers, captains of business, and entrepreneurs. I still had plenty of that fuel in me, but it was off by about 20 percent. I wasn't performing at capacity, and I knew something was up.

What was up was that I was developing attractions to men. And as I sensed these feelings, I began to feel "less than" my other male classmates. A secret was developing, and I hadn't had secrets before. I was organizing the "Ride for Life," and although I was able to do it despite the distraction, I didn't do it as well as I might have. In hindsight, I recognize that the full power of my creativity was not at work.

Over the next ten years, my life would play out in a way that would carry me far away from my real potential. The year was 1983. It was a very different time, both socially and politically—there wasn't much tolerance for homosexuality. A year earlier, I had been elected to the school board in Melrose, Massachusetts, and there were no openly gay or lesbian elected officials, like there are now. Since I was more fully coming to the realization that I was gay, I was also realizing that this fact wouldn't play well in the local Melrose paper if the school board found out. I could just picture them accusing me of trying to convert students to being gay. No, I knew that my dream of becoming a state senator, then governor, and then president, was over. That was it. I was disabled, and it seemed like it happened overnight. I was devastated, but I wasn't really even aware of it. I certainly didn't want to deal with the reality of being gay. I didn't want to face the feelings it created inside of me—those feelings of being a misfit.

The other kids at Harvard who had those kinds of high aspirations had a serious advantage over me. In my mind, they were good kids, and now I wasn't. My image of myself as president was always a pure one: I was going to help people; they were going to look up to me; I was going to be their Jimmy Stewart. That image was stained now, and to make matters worse, only *I* knew it. So, on top of my dream falling apart on me, it was falling apart in a state of isolation, where there really wasn't a soul I felt I could speak to about the oncoming demise of what I had pictured to be my life. I was living in a society that, at every level, was telling me that, simply because I was gay, I was a degenerate who was so far below the standards of good citizenship that no dream—let alone the presidency— was a dream that I deserved. And my parents, God bless them, had grown up in that same society, so it would be a few years before they could come to grips with it and help me.

My self-loathing was deeper and more cruel than words could ever describe. I had been indoctrinated by an intolerant society, and now I was believing the lies. I was completely disenfranchised from any kind of support, and I was cutting myself off from my essence; in fact, I was coddling its opposite. I was stumbling down the wrong path, and this is not an environment in which real dreams can manifest. It was an environment of extreme unkindness toward myself, and manifesting dreams requires tremendous self-love.

Have you ever been in a life situation that aroused similar feelings in you? Have you ever had secrets? Do you now? Do you know that they're secrets? What's the basis for them? What are you frightened of? Why do you keep them secret? What effect do they have on you?

After college I worked in the Massachusetts State Senate, and I was playing guitar at night in different clubs around the Boston area—sometimes even up in New Hampshire and Maine, too. After about a year, I was playing five or six nights a week and writing a lot of my own songs. I think that unconsciously, I was deciding that if I couldn't lead in politics, then perhaps I could lead through music. A lot of my songs were political, so I was deciding whether this would be my voice. It was a severe compromise for me, but I don't think I even realized it at the time.

I became obsessed with the idea of getting a record deal. I wanted to be the next Bruce Springsteen. I was so *not* Bruce Springsteen. It was so *not* the right dream. I was so *not* living my real life. This was not my destiny. This was not my calling. This was my agenda, my strategy—my fantasy—but it had none of the magic or resonance of a dream. If you're not following your destiny or your calling, you're not going to have your real dreams come true because in that context, real dreams cannot manifest. But I didn't know any of this; all I knew was that I wasn't going to get a record deal in Massachusetts. I didn't want to struggle in the jungle of New York, so I figured I'd move to California.

I packed up my car in April of 1985. I had my sound system and my guitar in the back, along with all my clothes and belongings, and about $1,000. My sister Nancy said she'd make the drive out there with me so I wouldn't be alone for five days, and then she'd fly back. I was sad, I was lonely, and I was hating myself. We left the driveway with a U-Haul storage container on the car's roof, and my mom and dad stood there waving good-bye. I didn't know what lay ahead of me, and I didn't know if I'd ever be back.

We rolled down the hill, and by the time we got to the corner—a hundred yards away—I already felt a million miles from home, and I missed everything about it. In a very real sense, I already *was* a million miles from my home, because my soul's home was that environment of dreaminess it was surrounded in as a child. While it may have seemed that I was headed to California to pursue a dream, somewhere my soul knew that I was taking it on the path to oblivion, and that we were only going to get farther away from home at every level.

Nancy flew back after a few days, and I set out on my ten-year journey to escape myself—then, finally, to find myself, which has taken another ten years. I worked as a waiter at a swanky French restaurant on Sunset Boulevard for three days until they fired me because I couldn't tell the snails from the clams, or the chicken from the veal. I tried another restaurant and got fired from there, too. I actually was able, somehow, to drop four slices of honeydew melon, one at a time, from the tray on my shoulder directly into the full coffee cup of a tourist wearing a brand-new dress. I tried selling encyclopedias for a few days in Watts. Over the years, I worked for different charities, helping them with their fund-raising; I played clubs here and there and spent all my money making demos and buying equipment. I almost completely lost touch with my classmates from college, but from the alumni magazine, I could see that all their hopes and dreams were becoming real—they were getting married, having kids, getting the Ph.D.'s and J.D.'s, and becoming doctors. And here I was, working these dead-end jobs, trying to write music, and getting rejected left and right from every record company.

At the same time, my credit was falling apart. I was late on my car payments, and then I defaulted on my student loan. After I first got to California, I was trying to borrow money from a friend of mine who had moved out from Boston and I ended up spending a few days living out of my car. Then there were times when I had to go into the change jar of the guy I was living with so I could have lunch at McDonald's. I had parking tickets, and my car got towed because I hadn't paid them. They wanted $600 to get my car back—I didn't even have $10. I remember feeling like I really wanted to jump off the ledge of my apartment building. Whoever that kid was that was a dreamer—man, he was gone, gone, gone . . . and I had no idea where to find him.

All throughout this time, I was becoming obsessed with certain romantic interests—gay men—but only the ones who I could tell would keep their emotional distance from me. I was pursuing the unattainable—chasing. If someone that I thought was attractive seemed a bit mysterious, or ambiguous about whether or not they were interested in me, I was hooked. If they told me they weren't really sure if they were straight or gay, the sheer fact that they thought they could go back to being straight made me feel *less* than them, because I knew *I* couldn't go back. Also, because I felt less than them, I wanted to have them around me. I was addicted to the pain of not being able to attain them. That pain became familiar to me, and since we, as human beings, tend to gravitate toward that which is familiar, I kept gravitating toward that kind of pain. If it seemed unavailable, I wanted it, because I was familiar with the pain of that disappointment. On the other hand, if someone showed serious interest in me, I would run away. I idealized people that I didn't know, and then I would pursue them. I would "fall in love" with people without knowing them. In retrospect, I can see that I had no idea what a true love, based on trust, mutual respect, cooperation, and compromise in a partnership, really meant. What I thought was love was yet another form of fantasy. I gravitated toward situations that would put me in emotional and psychological jeopardy, and these situations began to make my life unmanageable. If you were having a conversation with me, I was only half there. The other half of me was looping the "movie" of my obsession over and over again in my head.

Life was a sorry mess, and it wasn't getting any better.

The path I was on was all about escape, so I didn't have to face the darkness of my life, so I didn't have to face my feelings about being gay, my grief at the loss of the life I had planned, or the loss of my ideal of myself. I got addicted to the pain of being in relationships where I wasn't treated very well, and I was having a lot of sex on the side to numb that pain. There is a wonderful dedication in Charlotte Davis Kasl's book, *Women, Sex, and Addiction: A Search for Love and Power*, that says, "Dedicated to the hope that one day, whenever someone sees another human body, they also see a precious human soul." That certainly was the opposite of the philosophy I was living.

This began to completely destroy my self-image. During the day, I'd dress up in a suit to go to work, and I'd hobnob with all these affluent people who were being courted as major donors by the charities I represented. These people had families, were upstanding, and really liked and thought highly of me, but then when I'd go home, I had this horribly lonely existence that involved one meaningless sexual encounter after another to ease my pain. I was spiraling downward, and I didn't know a way out. So I would go out and have more sex—which created more pain. Ironically, I was using pain to numb pain, and I was using sex to numb the pain that was supposed to be distracting me from the deepest pain of all—the loss of my life, my ideals, and my dreams.

At the same time, I was losing friends to AIDS, and that made it all worse. Not only was the death of my spirit a reality, but there was real, physical death all around me. The list of people I knew who died of AIDS numbers well into the 30s. Most of them were only in their 20s and 30s. Good kids. Good people. We were killing ourselves spiritually and physically. Lucky for me, my self-loathing never ran quite so deep as to expose myself knowingly to AIDS, but I came close. I was nothing but damned lucky. Others weren't so lucky.

Chris, whom I had dated for several months, died when he was 27. Timmy—not much over 30. Rick—late 20s. Freddy. Bobby. Barry. Frank. Many others. I remember watching one friend in the hospital—for about 15 minutes, I watched his chest pump up and down with the rhythm of the life-support equipment. It was just him and me in the room, and I had to watch this brilliant man reduced to looking like an audio-animatronic robot with this awful mechanical sound and measured gusts of air coming out of his chest. He died a few days later. I spent lots of Saturday afternoons at Hollywood memorial services, with big blown-up pictures of these young heartthrobs, smiling for all of posterity—their mothers and fathers standing by the pool, often meeting their son's gay friends for the first time. It was awkward, yet comforting for them somehow. They got to see that we weren't all bad. They got to see that, in fact, we were pretty good people.

Then one day, in 1991, finally, after years of pain and confusion, surrender. After three or four years of wandering down this very dark path, I was diagnosed with hepatitis A. I was incredibly jaundiced and had been out of work for six weeks. I had been working for a famous scientific research institute based in Israel, doing fund-raising, and I hated the job. It was another one of those suffocating environments. I spent most of those six out-of-work weeks in tears, wondering how I'd ever gotten to this place. I didn't know that I had hepatitis A—at first I thought that maybe I'd contracted HIV or hepatitis B. I had hit a bottom—a great big, dark, deep bottom. Thank God. I was ready to surrender my agenda. It wasn't working anymore. It was killing me.

I decided to go into therapy. Two visits a week, faithfully, for ten years. I knew I wanted a *complete* therapy—I didn't want to Band-Aid a problem. I wanted a thorough understanding of myself. Session after session, over the years, I worked through every issue: Was I gay or was I straight? Why did I want to be president? Why was I running from my life? Why was I engaging in self-destructive behavior? Why was I attracted to people who didn't treat me well or who held me at arm's length? Why would I become emotionally dependent on people without even knowing them? Why would I stay in bad relationships? What were the things I made part of my personality that really belonged to others? What did I really want out of life?

Kris (my therapist) and I worked through everything, from every angle, in hundreds of hours of deep, honest sessions. When I walked into her office for the first time, I resolved right then and there that there would be no secrets—that I would tell her absolutely everything. I did. And I don't have any secrets in my life anymore. This was the first major step I took toward taking responsibility for my life.

Around the fifth year of therapy, I realized, with Kris's help, that I had two addictive patterns: I was addicted to bad relationships, and I was addicted to sex as a means of coping with the pain of it all. I decided to get into a miraculous 12-step program called Sex and Love Addicts Anonymous, based on the 12-step program of Alcoholics Anonymous. With the help of therapy and 12-step, I've returned to myself—to my essence. I now have great pride in myself, I respect myself, and I tell the truth. I don't have secrets—for a while, secrets were all I ever had.

Why have I told you all of this, and what does it have to do with understanding your destiny? I've told you these things about myself because what I learned from this process was that you can't even begin to contemplate your destiny if you're not confronting the reality of your life. My friend Ritch told me once about something very profound that he'd heard—a truth—that we have to be willing to give up our fantasies in order to have our dreams.

I used to want to be Bruce Springsteen. That was a fantasy— the thought of him filled me with a vicarious sense of responsibility. He seemed like a man who could be counted on. I don't want to be Bruce Springsteen anymore. I'm the man I always wanted to be. I can count on myself. I used to always look up to my dad as the essence of what a man should be. I still do, but now I feel like his equal; I don't feel shamed by a chasm of contrast, as I did for a long time. I have a lot of regard for who I am, for what I've done, and for the way in which I conduct myself. I have my life back, I have my dreams back, and I have my soul back. I'm back on my path. I've reclaimed that eight-year-old kid who was so full of energy, dreams, fun, and imagination. I've reclaimed that 17-year-old kid who used to look up at the clouds and just dream—carried away by the sheer limitlessness of it all. I've reclaimed my real life. I'm not self-destructive now. I'm self-actualized. Creativity flows in me. And I'm glad that I'm gay. If I weren't gay I may never have created the AIDSRides. I may never have gotten to create the magical career that Pallotta TeamWorks is for me now. Those things we try to avoid in life are often the very things that will lead us to our fulfillment. Those things that make us misfits are what also make us magic.

You have to be a whole person before you can begin the work of your dreams. I told the universe that I was ready to have my life back, and I worked my ass off to demonstrate my sincerity and resolve, and the universe has obliged—I have my life back, and I'm whole. And it's out of that wholeness that all my dreams have flowed. I'm not a stranger to love anymore. I'm not a stranger to life anymore. I'm not a stranger to myself anymore. "There's no place like home. There's no place like home. There's no place like home. . . ." Not long ago, I had a dream where a man came into a room singing those words in a prayer, with tears in his eyes. That man was me.

Do you have a suspicion about yourself and addiction? Is there a substance, a person, or a pattern that you're addicted to that's keeping you from your real self, your real life, and your real problems? Is there a pain to which you're addicted? A disappointment? Are you in an abusive relationship or job? Do you have any reason to believe that you abuse food, gambling, or money? Is there some other way in which you're avoiding your life and avoiding your destiny? Were you harmed in any way in your childhood? Do you know how you might begin to seek help? Is there someone you can talk to?

The More Life You Ask for, the More Life You'll Get

You can't see your destiny, or discover your calling, or hear the way the universe is pointing you if you're avoiding your life. I believe that God grants us our wishes—and God determines what our wishes are by our actions. If our actions take us away from our real lives, we're saying to God, "I don't want to see my destiny, and I don't want to live my real life." So God says, "Okay, then, I won't show it to you. Your wish is granted. You let me know when you're ready. Until then, I'll let you stay bored in your addictive patterns, or in your 'escape movie,' and nothing new, mysterious, or challenging will happen to you. If you ever change your mind, then just let me know. I'm always around."

In therapy (and in 12-step) I started to say to God that I was ready to live out my destiny. I wanted to understand my calling, my reason for being here. I was going to stop running. I was asking God, through my actions—by the things I was doing and by the things I was *not* doing—that I was ready for more of life. And God granted my wish. She started sending me my life, one chapter at a time, and the chapters started getting more and more interesting. In each chapter, my destiny was unfolding. Like a puzzle, the pieces were starting to come together, and I could see what it was that God wanted me to do—which was not very different from the impulses I had as a child. God wanted me to be of service, to help make the world a better place. She wanted me to build spaceships with pink curtains—and She was willing to send me tools and ideas and help.

To me, it's a lot like a video game. The more you practice and show up, and the more responsibility you take for the reality—not the fantasy—of your life, the more levels you're going to get to play, and they get more and more interesting, and more and more satisfying. But at any point, no matter how long you practice, you're ultimately faced with the choice of engaging your life or avoiding it; to the point that if you avoid it, your evolving path will be hidden from you—no matter how much therapy or 12-step work you've done. To the extent you open your arms, your path will continue to unfold and be shown to you.

Is there some way you're avoiding your life and your destiny? Is there something you haven't been confronting that you get defensive about? What negative "scripts" have you been running? What would it take for you to let go of these patterns? What is the payoff?

A good example of this is the way you can stay in a job you hate—a job that takes you to the antithesis of your essence—if you're simultaneously engaging in an addictive pattern that numbs the pain of it. But the minute you start to experience the pain—stop running from it—take responsibility for it—you're going to see just how *much* you hate your job, and then, you're really going to have to do something about it. Yet as it stands now, you can stay in a dead-end job for the rest of your life because you're not facing how much you hate it—and in that, you're doing your soul a tremendous disservice. You're telling God not to show you your life, so She's not. And She'll leave you in that dead-end job as long as you want Her to. It's not Her fault. She doesn't care. You're getting exactly what you asked for.

Again, your life before your calling—your destiny before your dreams. If you try to fulfill your dreams in a context where your life isn't happening, it's going to be an extremely frustrating and debilitating exercise. It simply doesn't work that way. You have to know who you are.

I spent all those years trying to get a recording contract, and in pursuing that goal, I tried to apply all of the things I knew about making dreams come true. But I had the wrong dream. Actually, I didn't really even have a dream at all. I just had a scheme—an agenda to avoid my real life—and my desire to get a record deal was just part of that avoidance. *If you have a scheme instead of a dream—if you're simply working an agenda that's yours and not God's, there's no amount of knowledge or effort that will make it come true—not in the way your soul is looking for it to come true.*

What your soul is looking for in pursuit of the impossible is a kind of happiness, a fulfillment that integrates some semblance of your path—your destiny. Anything else is going to drive you to drink, be miserable, or at the very least, be left with a vague feeling of a lack of fulfillment.

I used to come home from my dead-end job every day and go up into my loft and try to write songs . . . but my songs always sucked. I remember one song I wrote called "Limits." The refrain of the song said, "You've got to live within the limits," which was the exact opposite of how I really felt. When you're pursuing an agenda, instead of your destiny, you'll actually find yourself going down a road that's directly *opposite* of your true path.

At my best, I was good. But Springsteen, Joni Mitchell, and Bob Dylan are *great*. They are masters. This was their calling; it wasn't mine. They were signed to record deals when they were barely in their 20s. Their talent was there at a very young age. Mine was, too—I organized "Ride for Life" when I was 21. But I ran away from it, and I tried to create a different destiny. No amount of visualization, meditation, positive thinking, or attending "How to Get a Record Deal" seminars was going to make it the right dream, nor was I going to "make it happen."

How do you know when something is in this category? Believe me, you know. You may not want to admit it—and some people will go to their graves stuck to their agenda—but you know. First of all, you find yourself getting defensive when someone tells you that maybe you ought to try something else. If your soul is struggling, then that's a good sign that you're working an agenda, and not your real dream. Give yourself a break, and go get an ice cream.

Is there a dream you've been banging your head against the wall to achieve? Is it a dream or a scheme? Does it feel connected to your destiny, or is it just something you really want—or really think you want? Is the process beautiful to you or frustrating? Is it consistently frustrating?

Somewhere around 1986, still living in California, I even tried to hook up with some students back at Harvard and get another "Ride for Life" going. But it wasn't my calling or my destiny. I wasn't receiving any signal— I was just plain afraid. I was scrambling—there was rejection and failure all around me. This idea was all about control, all about trying to escape these horrible negative feelings. I remember trying to convince the Harvard students to hire me to take over the organizing of the fourth annual Ride. After all, I was the original creator of it. I thought for sure that it was a slam-dunk. *Of course they'll want me to take it over—I'm a celebrity to them,* I thought. It was a choice between me and this other guy from Stanford who was organizing similar events, and he wanted to fold the "Ride for Life" into his organization. I flew back to Boston and pleaded my case with the undergraduates who were now in charge. The other guy made his case, too. He won. I was angry and resentful and devastated.

Those kids weren't buying my agenda. They knew that I wasn't right for the job—that it wasn't my destiny—that I was somehow reaching back into the past to try to find some visionary that I used to be. But they were telling me flat out that "he" did not exist in the past, that he existed in the present, and this was not the place where I was going to find him. I didn't like their answer. I was confused by it. It wasn't what I wanted to hear. I felt as if I couldn't get the dream to come true. But the truth was simply that I couldn't get my *agenda* to come true— my newest fantasy.

This book is not about how to make any arbitrary self-willed fantasy come true. It's about having your *dreams* come true. It's about going down the path you were meant to follow—taking responsibility for your life and all its joys, problems, and sorrows—laying the groundwork so that when your moment comes, you'll recognize it, and you'll have the tools to manifest it. Don't run from yourself. Don't be a stranger to yourself. Get beyond your fantasies so you can arrive at your dreams. Be the dreamer you were meant to be.

Chapter Three

Understanding Your Calling

A Story about the Call to Kindness

I volunteer at a hospital for children, and there's an 11-year-old girl there whom I'll call Maureen for confidentiality purposes. She's a stunning African-American girl—she has a beautiful face and carries herself with tremendous dignity and poise. I can picture her being a senator or Secretary General of the United Nations one day. Unfortunately, Maureen has sickle-cell anemia.

A few months ago we were playing, and it got to be 7:30, which is the time the hospital's playroom closes. She asked Sara, the staff supervisor, if Danny (as she calls me) could come "visit me in my room after the playroom closes." Sara said that I was just a volunteer and that 7:30 was my time to leave, so if I was going to stay later it would have to be up to me. I overheard this and decided that I'd go visit Maureen in her room after we got the playroom cleaned up. So I did, and she was in her bed watching TV and playing with one of her dolls. She was really happy to see that I'd come by. We enjoy each other—we have a lot of fun together, and we joke with each other really well. I asked her a question about how long she'd be in the hospital this time and she said she didn't know. I asked her how long she'd been sick, and I wasn't prepared for her answer. She said to me, "All my life." She'd been diagnosed when she was less than a year old.

We talked. She asked me if I'd unpackage her new Barbie Doll, which I did. Geez, they put a lot of wires around those things in the box. I brushed Barbie's hair for her, and then she asked me to look in her little plastic change purse to see if I thought she had enough money in there to buy a "Big and Tasty" burger at the McDonald's downstairs. It looked like she had about four dollars, so I told her she had enough. But I asked her why she was going to eat at McDonald's—hadn't the hospital fed her? She said they'd come by with food, but she wasn't hungry at the time. I asked her how she'd get down to the McDonald's, and she said one of the nurses would take her down later.

So we talked a bit more, and I said I'd have to be going, and she asked, "Do you have to? Can't you stay just a little longer?" She didn't have any visitors, so I decided I'd stay and we'd play and talk a little longer. I left about 15 minutes later, and as I was walking down the hall, a voice in my head said, "Go get her a 'Big and Tasty.'" Then that other voice popped up and rebutted, "Aw, c'mon—you haven't eaten all day, you're starving yourself, she has a nurse who'll go down there and get it anyway. Don't run a guilt trip on yourself here—don't be a martyr—just go home and grab yourself some dinner before you faint, and Maureen will be just fine. You did enough already."

I started to wonder, What would Alan do? (Alan was a very special person in my life, and I'll tell you all about him, and the meaning of that question, later on in this chapter.) Damn. As soon as I asked myself that, I was on my way downstairs to buy her the "Big and Tasty." I got her fries and a milkshake, too. I came back upstairs and knocked on her door and said, "Surprise!" She tilted her head down, raised her eyes up, and slowly said, "You're the best person in the whole world. How can I ever repay you?"

Well, those words melted me—that alone made it all worth it. I insisted that she get back into bed, and I pretended I was a fancy French waiter—I got her tray all set up right, laid all of her food out just so, and then I had to wait to watch her take one big, juicy bite out of that "Big and Tasty." Somehow, watching her enjoyment as all of her taste buds were triggered by that first bite, I was getting enjoyment out of it myself. Maureen was happy, and so I was happy, too, and I felt, that I was living out a calling—a calling to be kind.

This chapter is about putting your calling before your dreams. Throughout this chapter, I'm going to ask you an important question, which is: *What is your life about?* What moves you? What do you want them to put on your gravestone? Again, *what is your life about?* Out of the honest answer to this question, your dreams will flow. It's not a question that you have to force yourself to answer; it's a question you have to be willing to live with. Live the question, *What is my life about?* and, like a satellite dish, the answers will come to you. You'll find yourself living the answer. You don't have to go out and grab the answers. But to keep the question alive in your life is to have the satellite dish turned on—that's all you have to do.

Have you ever experienced those moments when you're watching one of those get-rich-quick infomercials, and you keep watching it and watching it, to the point where you're almost ready to buy the videotape? You begin to convince yourself that all you ever really wanted was to get rich, as if getting rich alone could actually make you happy.

When you start getting frustrated, you feel like you have no direction in life, and you're wandering from idea to idea, it's because you're out of touch with a sense of why you're here—you're pursuing an agenda that's been born of your pride, ego, fear, or insecurity, and it has nothing to do with your real destiny. You think you're not successful enough. You're worried about what people think; you're afraid that your potential will pass you by if you don't take control. Sure, these things will motivate you, but they motivate you to some quick, face-saving enterprise that lacks the grace and dignity of your true calling.

Imagine Gandhi trying to pursue his dreams without a sense of his destiny. It's comical. I mean, how on earth would he have a sense of his dreams without a sense of his destiny? There's that saying that a person who *stands* for nothing will *fall* for anything. Picture this Gandhi—a Gandhi with no sense of his path in life: "Well, maybe I could open a car dealership. No, no, that's not really the business I'd like to be in . . . Real estate—that's it! Real estate! I could make a lot of money in real estate. But I don't know if that's what I want. Maybe I'll be a dancer. That would be a nice, simple existence. I've always liked to dance. I'm really very creative. Maybe that's what I'll do. Actually, I have this idea for a new juice machine. Maybe I could do a juice machine informercial. I could get a lot of money and then start a foundation."

How does one get a sense of why they're here? Well, you have to listen. You have to listen to what God is telling you to do and to what God is telling you not to do. You have to watch the way the universe is pointing you, and you have to watch the way it isn't. Billy Joel has a line in one of his songs that goes, "You can linger too long in your dreams." There was a period in my life when that line haunted me. "How can you linger too long in your dreams?" I'd ask myself. "Aren't dreams all about persistence? Isn't that what all the power motivation books say?" Not always. Sometimes persistence can be about stubbornness, and that's the opposite of following your path and your real dreams. Stubbornness, in the face of obvious signs being shown to you by God and the universe, is nothing to which you want to aspire. Believe me, I know. Being stubborn is to close your ears and eyes to the messages from beyond so that you can pursue your own agenda—but you need your ears and eyes to see and hear your destiny.

It's not tricky to tell the difference between when you're being stubborn and when you're being persistent. It's only tricky if you're so committed to being stubborn that it blinds you. Then you get what we call *confused*: "I'm so confused I don't know what to do with my life." There's an old Eastern adage that says that confusion and boredom are the guardians of the truth. So watch out if you're confused or bored. You're shielding yourself from your own truth. You're not really confused—you're just using confusion to hold you back from your true path as a way to keep from facing up to some hard realities. If you really take a look at it, it's not tricky, because the signs will be all over the place.

Is there anything that's been confusing you for a long time? Do you lack direction in life? Is it confusing to you? Do you feel that you're without a path or destiny? How long have you felt this way? How often do you stop to just listen to your inner voice?

How Do You Uncover Your Calling?

If you want to discover your calling, you have to listen and you have to look. But that's not always as easy as it sounds. What are you looking and listening for? Well, you're looking and listening for the answers to some questions: *Who are you? Who is the person you want to be? What is that person like? What are your ideals? What are your values? What is your life about?* To me, these are the great questions.

You can get some practice answering the deeper questions by asking some simpler ones first, such as: *What do you like?* Live with that question for a while. In fact, it might be useful to live with that question all the time.

One night, I had friends coming over for dinner, and I was trying to pick out the right CDs to put in the CD changer. My thought process went something like, *Well, let's see, Annie Lennox is cool and everyone likes her, so I'll put that in there. I'll put this* Glory of Gershwin *in there because some of my gay friends won't think I'm gay enough or have enough style if I don't have some kind of classic show thing or something in there, so that will make me look good. Sting—everyone likes Sting, and* Fields of Gold *is mellow—it doesn't have any real rockers that are going to be too loud and offend anyone or make them think I have no taste in dinner music, and Deep Forrest would be good for everyone—that creates the right mood.* So this is what went on in my head—I wasn't even conscious that the voices were that active.

I have a friend named Ignacio, who, like me, loves Bruce Springsteen. Ignacio also loves Frank Sinatra. In fact, the only singers he really likes are Springsteen and Sinatra. Consequently, whenever you go over to his house for dinner or whatever, guess what you hear on the CD player? Springsteen and Sinatra. It's all you *ever* hear. He plays what he likes. It's actually very endearing and sort of cute. It gives him a certain sense of personality that's refreshingly different from everyone else's homogenized presentation to the world. It doesn't dawn on him to be concerned about how he'll look to everyone for just playing Springsteen and Sinatra.

So, I know that I like model rockets. I also know that I like orange sherbet, pizza, and fried clams. I like being creative, and I like to play the harmonica. I don't like managing people. These realizations are more important than the things you learn in a cave in the Himalayas, because they allow you to be *yourself.* And when you relax enough to see yourself at the level of the surface, you can begin to see yourself at the level of great depth.

What are the simple things you like? Who is it that you're trying to be in life that isn't really you? What is it you're trying to like for the sake of others that you don't really like yourself?

Live with these questions. By answering these questions in some detail on a regular basis, you can develop confidence—and really believe that getting to know yourself is actually achievable.

Going Deeper

Identifying the simple things is the easy part. How do you get to the deeper issues? How do you get to know your calling? First, let the universe know that you're ready. Second, simply don't do anything that's designed to take you away from the hard issues in your life. We must confront our lives head-on, with integrity, courage, and responsibility, but that's no small task. Self-knowledge requires inquiry, work, and practice. You can't get there with the brief advice I've just given. I lack the knowledge to lead you on such a pursuit, and even if I had it, it's a subject way too big to tackle here—in fact, I don't really think that *any* book or even any *series* of books could come close to seriously aiding you with the task. But I can relate to you the tools that I've used to help me in my own search.

I'm guided by three essential disciplines: (1) spirituality; (2) what I call "inspiration curriculum"; (3) and self-knowledge—pretty much in that order. Spirituality is my relationship to a power infinitely greater than my mind or myself. Inspiration curriculum is material—books, experiences, and teachers that support my ability to receive dreams and see imaginative, outrageous possibilities. Self-knowledge is an understanding of the "automaticity" of my mind and my reactions, eventually leading to the uncovering of pieces of my true, unautomated self. I've made whatever progress I have toward this end in psychotherapy. Each of these three essential disciplines is a manifestation of the question *What is my life about?*—they're each evidence to God and to the universe that I'm asking that question, and my satellite dish is turned on. They're each evidence that I'm seeking, and to the degree that the universe believes that I'm honestly asking the question, it will feed me the answer.

I'm a huge believer in the value and intelligence of psychotherapy as a tool for living and dreaming, and I don't believe that there's a person who couldn't benefit from it. As I said, I stayed with the same therapist faithfully for ten years. I knew when I entered therapy that I didn't just want some help for a few months in getting through a tough time. I wanted to understand my whole self. I set a goal of having a complete therapy and I achieved it, and I really came to know myself. I would not have accomplished most of the things I have without it.

There are so many things out there now that offer the "instant fix." There are countless self-help books that give the impression that the thesis contained within is the answer, and that once you've finished the book you're ready for a fabulous life. I don't think it's that easy—I think it takes *years*. Remember how I said in the Introduction that I felt there was a basic set of principles that applies to making your dreams come true, and that in the absence of this knowledge you'll be at a severe disadvantage in trying to make them come true? Well, similarly, there are laws that apply to understanding oneself. People spend years and years practicing to become great baseball players, yet we're expected to become great human beings without any practice. Understanding yourself takes a big commitment, a lot of study, and constant practice—it can't be accomplished by a self-help book here and there, or a weekend seminar now and then.

I also think that it's impossible to self-teach all this. Imagine trying to become a doctor without any teachers and without any books. Yet people think they can come to understand themselves by "thinking about things," or trying to "sort things out" on their own. It's a fantasy, if you ask me. Our minds and behaviors are complex and elusive. I've never even heard of anyone who can structure time in such a way that they're actually able to methodically "sort through" thoughts and problems and arrive at some enlightenment without the help of trained professionals. It's a vacuum there inside our heads. It's virtually impossible to figure things out without the aid of trained professionals experienced in the art of self-knowledge, and without the aid of a structured process in which to do the examination.

Beyond some kind of therapy, a spiritual path is important. It's important for me so that I remain humble and don't go too far down the path of thinking that everything I've accomplished is a testament to me. It's a testament to God. It helps me avoid the trap of following my own agenda instead of the plan that God has mapped out for me. In my own 12-step work, I try to attend at least two meetings a week, and I talk to the people I sponsor a few times a week in addition to that. I also pray and do walking meditations, but I'm not as disciplined about that as I'd like to be. The point is, I have to dedicate *time* to my spiritual life. If I don't, life goes flat.

There was a time, back in those dark days of my 20s, when I thought I was a spiritual person. Someone would ask me, "Are you spiritual?" and I would say, "Oh yeah, I'm really spiritual," but the truth was that I just *wanted* to be spiritual. I wasn't actually dedicating any time to my spiritual path. We need time with God—quiet time in Her presence—in order to be more aware of Her will for us, and so we'll be more fully able to listen and to see. The periods when I devote time to God are the most beautiful in my life—the times when I don't are often the most painful.

In addition to therapy and my spiritual path, for me, it's important to remain a student of possibility. When I was 19 years old, I did the *est* training, and I was very involved with an enterprise called the Hunger Project, which taught me a great deal about the power of commitment and about the realm of possibility. On a regular basis, through participating in Pallotta TeamWorks' own events, or through reading, I expose myself to things that will teach me more about how impossible things get accomplished. Every year now, I participate in at least one of our events. It's important for me, on a regular basis, to place myself in difficult and demanding circumstances to take myself out of my comfort zone, because it's only in those places that I'm reminded of my real potential. I'm reminded that there's a more interesting, more capable me that lives outside of the comforts of home, and that, if I want to continue to discover him, then from time to time I must go to those remote places where he lives.

So, a warning here: This book will not produce miracles. It's not powerful enough to propel your life into a new realm of dreams fulfilled and great peace and happiness. It will have virtually no lasting impact on you. Once you put it down, much of what you have read you'll forget, and you'll forget it quickly. However, if this book inspires you to dedicate yourself to a process, whereby you keep these kinds of lessons around you all the time and begin to dedicate yourself to self-exploration, then someday, maybe, you'll see changes in your life. You'll see your calling coming clear, and your dreams coming true.

Looking for Clues to Your Calling

I think that our callings just *are*—they exist within us. Distinct from the matter of finding something that's missing, our calling is something that we simply have to come to know by observing ourselves and observing the things to which we are drawn and the things about which we become impassioned. Again, it's not something that needs to be coerced or forced. It's there already, and comes to us very naturally and easily.

First Clue—Heroes

Growing up in Boston in the 1960s, I was very influenced by the messages of John and Robert Kennedy and Martin Luther King, Jr. The boldness of speaking about going to the moon, the compassion in Kennedy's Inaugural Address when he spoke about "the poor people in the huts and villages of half the globe"—these things felt visionary, right, moral, and purposeful to me. Robert Kennedy's dream of a "new world society," and his statement that "each of us would ultimately judge ourselves on the extent to which we would help create that"—these things seemed full of vitality, hope, and energy to me as a young person. These messages were wholly distinct from anything any other adults were saying, and they really captivated me. They resonated with me, and there was nothing I needed to do to make them resonate. They still do.

Who were your heroes? Whom did you admire, and why?

Second Clue—Social Justice Lists

I also have vivid recollections of sitting at the Sunday dinner table as a kid. All my relatives were there, and they would talk about everything that was wrong with our country and with the world. They would talk about how the working-class guy was getting killed with taxes, how bad the government was, how bad Nixon was, and how the welfare system was a mess. They would go on and on. Meanwhile, little eight-year-old me was making lists of all the things I was going to have to fix when I grew up. I can't believe it today—I actually used to make lists of the world's problems when I was a kid. "Okay, I have to make sure that taxes get lower for construction workers, I have to fix the welfare system, I have to fix the government, and I have to be a better leader than Nixon."

Were you concerned about the world around you as a kid? Were you concerned about the environment, your neighborhood, or the things you heard on the news?

Third Clue—Rooting for the Underdog

There were other influences on me as well. I realize now that I identify with the underdog; in many ways, I always considered my dad—who was a construction worker—an underdog. There were a lot of times when he would be laid off—either because someone else was close to the business agent, or simply because the New England dirt in winter was too frozen to dig or pour concrete. Sometimes he'd be laid off around the holidays, and I remember him being very down about it. I didn't like seeing my dad being at the mercy of more powerful influences. It seemed unjust to me that a guy who only wanted to take good care of his family was being thwarted by influences outside his control. I became loyal to the underdog and began to hate any kind of injustice. It was an extremely formative influence in me, and it has a lot to do with the choices that I made. It helped to shape my calling in a lot of ways.

Did you root for the underdog as a kid? Do you still today? To whom were you loyal? What influenced you?

Fourth Clue—Creativity and Marketing

When I was in elementary school, I used to draw logos all the time. I loved to draw the logos for 7-Up, Necco, STP, Sinclair—you name it. It was in therapy that I was able to recall the magnitude of my creativity in childhood. I was also able to get in touch with how much I loved the visual elements of a great advertisement. I loved the way a particular font looked—I was hooked on fonts. I don't know why. It's in my DNA. I began to see how much I loved graphic design, and how much I loved music and the emotion it creates—especially when it's combined with visual elements in a good documentary, movie, or commercial. I began to realize that what I really liked about political campaigning was the marketing side of it. I loved marketing—and still do.

Even when I was a kid, cutting lawns and shoveling snow in the neighborhood, I used to market my services in a ways that went way beyond what the other kids would do. In that sense, I was a little bit of a misfit. I used to go to the graphic design supply store and buy all of these different Letraset rub-on fonts. I'd make these cool flyers with what I thought were clever headlines, and I would wrap the body copy around the headlines—just like I saw in the real magazine ads. The neighbors must have thought I was a nut. I mean, I was only 12, and here I was doing all this crazy marketing: "I Have a New Snowblower!" Like they really cared. "Are You Tired of a Messy Lawn?" They probably were tired of *me*. But advertising resonated with me, which also informed me about my innate calling.

Marketing and advertising is now a critical part of Pallotta TeamWorks', and it's one of the aspects of our business that I love the most. I thrive on creating great ads for our events—I love working with our creative staff on concepts and ideas. The marketing enthusiasm is integrated with my passion for social justice, and it's a wonderful, powerful combination. But I didn't have to go out and "find" these things—they were there all along.

What kinds of things did you doodle in school while you were daydreaming? What kinds of things did you draw as a kid? Did you sing? Skip? Dance? What did you do every day without even thinking about it? What did your childhood tell you your life should be about?

Fifth Clue—Bringing People Together

I can also see how much I've always enjoyed bringing people together. Perhaps that was because of the warmth and nurturing I felt growing up in a large, close Italian family. We were always together—there were always young people mixed with old people; food all over the place; the smell of baked stuffed shells, ricotta cheese, and tomato sauce; and crowded rooms with lots of conversation. I was always trying to convince my friends to come out and play and do things together—I liked big groups and big street hockey games.

I was always organizing events in my neighborhood, and was always opening lemonade stands. One summer night, my friends and I put together this great big neighborhood cookout. The flyer said:

"It's a hamburger and hot dog stand for the whole family."

(Compare this with the first line of our current AIDSRide materials—'The Ride is for everyone.' It's amazing to me to see the similarity 30 years later.)

Anyway, the flyer continued, *"Mothers and wives, get away from those hot stoves! Bachelors or husbands with wives that get in late* (see me trying to capture every demographic?)*, put those frozen dinners back in the freezer and come get some food that isn't in a sectional tin plate with 'Swanson' indented on the bottom. Kids, get away from the spinach and beef stew and come grab a good old American hot dog. There's plenty of food for the whole family, so come and enjoy. There'll be hamburgers, hot dogs, French fries, soft drinks, lemonade, Italian ice, and more—all at low prices* (there's the salesman in me). *Come and get it on Wednesday, August 25th at 5:30. Extra! You'll also get a chance to see the nut who did up this circular!!"* Sponsored by Dan Pallotta and Dean Bruno.

Did you grow up in a big or a small family? How did it influence you? Do you like to be around a lot of people, or are you more comfortable on your own?

Adding Up the Clues

All of these things: the desire to do bold and moral things, the desire to fix society's problems, the loyalty to the underdog, the love of creativity and marketing, the desire to bring people together—all of which were with me as a child—have converged and coalesced to form my life today. In each of them I can see the early signs of my calling. What would a kid who had all these different passions create when he grew up? Well, he'd create Pallotta TeamWorks, but how was I supposed to know that then? These days, Pallotta TeamWorks utilizes a Mobile City^{SM}, which brings thousands of people together, and uses giant mobile kitchens and refrigerators to feed them hot dogs, hamburgers, lemonade, and lots more. I use the spoken word, like my idols did, to try to inspire people to social action. I use my creativity and marketing skills to create social justice advertising campaigns that will bring people to our events. Our events raise money to help the underdogs in our society. And it's all becoming part of a strategic plan at Pallotta TeamWorks to use bold citizen action on a serious scale to solve some of the world's most pressing social problems—to try to cross things off that list I was making at the Sunday dinner table. It's truly amazing to me to see that my childhood was foretelling my future, and my calling was all right there. There is a clear alignment with the very earliest signs of my destiny on every level.

When you're in alignment with your calling, it's as fun as being a kid again. We recently finished two days of meetings on the master plan for our new Mobile City, in which all of our event structures, which are currently large military-type tents, will become these very innovative, morphing, sustainable, mobile structures on wheels that can be trucked from event to event under their own power. It's like a giant Lego set we're playing with, all in the name of ending AIDS, breast cancer, suicide, domestic poverty, and more. Right before that, I got to design a new commercial for MTV spotlighting our AIDS Vaccine Rides, and then I got to devise new ads that were going to run in *Rolling Stone, Vanity Fair,* and *National Geographic Adventurer* magazines. It's like being a kid, but with great big adult toys.

You already have a calling. It will manifest out of all of the things for which you have a talent. It may not fit into a box that looks like someone else's calling, so you may not think you have one. You may just have to create a box that's never existed before—one that's just for you.

All of the things that influenced me as a kid still influence me today. The most significant is probably the empathy for the underdog. I see the people of Africa as the underdogs. It seems unjust to me that they're dying of AIDS in such huge numbers in a world that could more than take care of them. The fact that there are political elements who would deny gays and lesbians the right to work, marry, or even be together also makes my blood boil. The fact that 41 percent of people in Los Angeles are living close to the poverty line incenses me. Underserved women with undetected breast cancer—the small charity trying to make a difference in the world without enough money to do it—they're underdogs to me, and they stir something deep and old and young all at the same time within me.

When I lose my footing, I go back to the question: *What is my life about?* The answer always comes up as some form of helping people—helping people in need, helping the underdog—and I'm once again guided.

What guides you? What evidence do you have of your own calling? What is your life about?

With Your Calling, You Create an Original Life

What I'm talking about requires a great deal of patience and tremendous faith. The waiting can be difficult and can feel lonely. What wants to manifest in you is a truly original life, and this is very uncommon. This is not what most people do—most people run quickly to the safe harbor of the common. There isn't a lot of agreement, understanding, or sympathy for an original approach out there. People will disapprove—you can bet on it.

The patience it all requires can be tough. You'll watch others who are on a more conventional path whiz right by you. They might be able to buy a house before you do. They might be having children before you do. Sometimes you'll feel like you're watching your life pass you by, with all of your potential strapped to the top of it. Combine that with the pressure of people waiting and watching to see when you're going to fail, and it can be very tempting to conform and abandon that seed of imagination in you. You have to be careful not to jump into something conventional out of fear. Your calling is there. If you protect it and remain true to it—your destiny will unfold.

You have to be willing to create an original life. I say this a lot when I'm speaking to college students. Most callings tend to manifest as very idiosyncratic hybrids of a variety of talents and passions, and they converge with one another to create unimaginable originality—a life that's unique and fresh in every way, and completely distinct from convention. It's completely different from anything anyone has ever created. It won't fit into a box—it will invent a new box that no one else will ever be able to fill. If it's original enough, you'll actually observe others trying to re-create your box. The need for patience arises, though, because it takes years for such a wonderful life to define itself, even preliminarily, and it's never fully defined. The truly original life is a life always in progress, always headed into the unknown.

Because it will be something that never existed, you won't be able to describe to anyone what it is you're trying to do, and because of that, you'll face great pressure to conform. Society knows only boxes, and they'll want to know which box to put you into, and you won't be able to tell them. This can be frustrating and painful. You'll feel weird, strange— sometimes even like you're being irresponsible because you're not choosing one of the boxes society currently has available.

I often ask college students to imagine Walt Disney at the age of 16 trying to explain to his parents, grandparents, teachers, and elders what his plans were for his life: "Well, I have this mouse, y'see . . . and I think he has a lot of potential." This was the situation he was actually in. "Yeah . . . I drew this mouse, and I think that it could turn into a multibillion-dollar international industry that will, in one lifetime, forever alter the fabric of popular culture." This was the *actual* dilemma Walt Disney found himself in as a teenager, although he wouldn't have been aware of it. Again, that's part of the problem—before the dream unfolds, you don't know what it's going to look like. It takes tremendous faith and courage to stick with your calling in those moments, when all the conventional forces of the world are stacked against you, pressuring you to conform. Walt Disney did not end up fitting into the box called "cartoonist." He ended up creating a new box called "theme park" that no one before had ever imagined. But it went beyond that—way beyond even that because "Disney" is so much more than even cartoons and theme parks. It's uniquely *Disney,* and it's the result of the convergence of 100 different qualities that were uniquely Walt Disney's own.

Think about Oprah Winfrey as a kid. Imagine her trying to explain to her parents or teachers that, instead of going to college to become an accountant, let's say, she wanted to create a media empire that would broadcast her ideals to the world. Can you imagine how silly she had to feel holding on to a vision that somewhere, deep in the recesses of her heart, she could be that huge? Can you imagine her trying to explain it?

Bruce Springsteen talks about how his father used to hate his guitar and long hair. He tells a story of how he came home late one night when he was a teenager and his father was waiting for him in the kitchen. As Bruce tells it, his dad asked him to sit down, and asked him, "What do you think you're doing with yourself?" Springsteen goes on to say that "the worst part about it was that I could never explain it to him."

Somewhere inside Bruce Springsteen's soul there was a knowing that he was up to something incredible, but how could that 19-year-old kid ever have envisioned what the words "Bruce Springsteen" would become—what they would represent? How could he have possibly foreseen the glory of the originality, depth of life, and success toward which he was headed? There was no way to explain or see it, so he was left feeling stupid in that moment. He couldn't articulate it. He probably felt like a misfit, and he probably thought, in his darker moments, that there was something wrong with that. He didn't have the gumption to say, "I'm going to be the future of rock-and-roll."

Jon Landau, a Boston rock reporter who later became Springsteen's manager, wrote exactly that about Springsteen in the '70s—"I have seen the future of rock and roll, and it is Bruce Springsteen." It's a tragedy that those who are on the road to creating the most beauty are the ones who often feel the most stupid on the early steps of their paths. But this is the price we pay for dreaming. It's a great price, but it's a great reward, too. If you feel silly about holding on to your ideals, don't despair— you're in dignified company. You're also in very fun company.

You know how they say that no two snowflakes are alike or that no two fingerprints are the same? It's the same with destiny. No two destinies are the same, so do yourself a favor and don't try to fit into one of society's boxes. You don't have to be a lawyer or go to graduate school in the next 15 minutes. Even if you decide to be a lawyer, who says you have to be the same kind of lawyer as everyone else? Why can't you take your love for the law, and your love for, perhaps, juggling, and become the general counsel to a circus? Now wouldn't that be fun? Have the patience and faith to allow your own unique calling to come to light.

Have you tried to conform in some way for someone else? Who? Why? Were you ever afraid that it just wouldn't all come together in a way that would make sense? What were you afraid of? Were you afraid of being left behind? Is there something in your heart that you want to do or be but you just can't explain it to anyone? If you tried, what would you start to say? Take an awkward stab at it, and just say it. Did you stop pursuing something because it wouldn't come together in a way that would fit in a traditional box? What are the things you're very good at? Are there things you're better at than anyone you know? Are there things you can do that no one else can do?

The Call to Service

As we seek our callings, we cannot divorce ourselves from the world in which we live. Try as we might to deny these surroundings in our minds, our hearts can still see. Our hearts know that there are children who will needlessly die in the next hour. We live in a world where approximately 25 million human beings will die of hunger and hunger-related diseases in the next 12 months alone—two-thirds of them children. That breaks down to 50 people in the next minute—a person in the next second. We live in an America where, in the last 15 years, more than half a million people have committed suicide. According to the FBI, in the United States in one year alone, more than 16,900 people were murdered, and more than 1,500,000 violent crimes were committed, including more than 93,000 rapes.

There are currently some 34.3 million people infected with HIV worldwide. At least 30 million are the poorest of the world's poor, living on less than two dollars a day. The miracle drugs known as protease inhibitors, widely available in the United States, are far too expensive and complicated for the poor nations of the world. Of the total worldwide cases, 23 million are in sub-Saharan Africa. There are 16,000 new HIV infections every day in the world. That's right—16,000 every day. Many of the countries affected, such as Botswana, Tanzania, and Namibia, have seen the life expectancies of their people plummet as a result of the predictions of the AIDS death toll.

The president of Botswana recently warned of the oncoming extinction of his people. Life expectancy there, which reached as high as 62.5 years in 1990, has dropped to less than 35 because of AIDS. According to Nelson Mandela, one out of every two young people in South Africa will die of AIDS. Approximately 450,000 Americans have died of AIDS since the onset of the disease—in Africa, 13 million have died. The death toll will be worse than the black plague—and it will occur swiftly, probably within ten years. During that time, some 20 million people will die, and in the absence of a vaccine, another 50 million will become infected. Already some 11 million African children wander their dusty village streets parentless, homeless, and vulnerable to horrific exploitation. On this continuing human journey into the 21st century, even more people are being left behind than in 1983 when we first did our cross-country bike ride. *This is the world in which we live.*

These things are hard to hear, and we live in a world that shuns sorrow and sadness. We embrace only what's positive and "upbeat." We tell the sorrowful to "lighten up." We coddle the positive, and we shun the negative—probably because if we were to open ourselves to the true sorrow we feel, we would be overcome by such a deep sadness that we might never stop crying.

But, out of that uncontrollable weeping, we might just find the motivation to say, "This must stop. This is not acceptable to my own values, my own ethics, and my own sense of compassion for people." Your sorrow can motivate you. I encourage you, in asking the question, *What will my life be about?,* to let in the true sorrow that you feel for the poor and the suffering. Because that's the world they live in, and, like it or not, that's the world we live in with them. You have it in you to be a hero—you've always wanted to be.

You have never, in your heart, wanted anything more. Our hearts know that there are little three-year-old AIDS orphans in Africa wandering the streets—and a dream is all about finding out what's in your heart. It's crucial that you listen to it at every level, in all of its dimensions. You don't need a speech to pump you up. You just need your sorrow. Robert F. Kennedy once said something that was so important to me I memorized it:

The fourth danger, my friends, is comfort. The temptation to follow the easy and familiar path so grandly spread before those of us with the privilege of an education. But that is not the path history has marked out for us. There is a Chinese curse that says, "May he live in interesting times." Well, like it or not, we live in interesting times. They are times of great danger and uncertainty, but they are also the most creative times in the history of mankind, and each of us will ultimately judge ourselves on the effort we have contributed to creating a new world society, and the extent to which our ideals and goals have helped shape that effort.

My dad earned his living as a construction worker, operating heavy equipment—backhoes, Gradalls, and front-end loaders. I remember him showing me some writing he'd done once, probably 20 years ago, which said that ever since he was young, he had a dream to find a way (when he had the time and money) to do something to help people. I was very moved, because I had never known this about him. I was touched that my dad revealed this to me—it took a willingness to be vulnerable. It really felt like he was revealing his lifelong dream to me. During the thousands and thousands of hours he spent out in the cold on construction sites, he held this dream of helping people in his heart. And the truth is, I think that dream is in the hearts of a lot of people.

Would you say that making the world a better place is one of your desires? Are you concerned about any of the world's problems? Which ones? What cause has always touched you? Why? Do you believe you could do something to make a difference?

What to Live About

Not knowing what to dream about is truly a function of not being clear about what to live about. You see, if what's in your heart is to help people, but you get brainwashed into thinking that your dream has to be about money, things might be less joyous and fulfilling for you than they could be under circumstances that resonate more fully with you. Your dream, which is really your *scheme*, is going to be very dissatisfying to you, even if you do reach it.

Not long ago, I read about a woman who was fed up with campaign financing in the United States, so she walked across America over the course of 14 months to make a statement about this. She was quoted in the *L.A. Times* on March 1, 2000, saying of her trip, "Along my 3,000 miles through the heart of America . . . did I meet anyone who thought that their voice as an equal citizen now counts for much in the corrupt halls of Washington? No, I did not. Did I meet anyone who felt anger or pain over this? I did, indeed, and I watched them shake with rage sometimes when they spoke, and I saw tears well up in their eyes."

Her name is "Granny D" Haddock, and she's 90 years old. Apparently she has emphysema *and* arthritis. This is a woman who knows what to live about, and consequently, she knows what to dream about.

The question *What is my life about?* gives me back my rudder, my chart, and my course in life. And it reminds me that what I want isn't to get rich or to have a bunch of stuff, but to be of service in some way. That doesn't mean I can't have the finer things in life—in fact, I do—but I didn't get these nice things by pursuing them. I went after my heart's desire—my commitment to service—and the money came along. But it's never been at the top of my list.

I believe that service is at the top of the list in everyone's heart. I believe that everyone wants their life to matter. Now this doesn't mean you have to join the Peace Corps or organize a cross-country bike ride to fight hunger. But it does mean that you have to find out what your true heart's desire is—not your ego's, your heart's. And if you really find that, it will be of service, even though it may not appear so on the surface. To be a great ballerina is a service to humanity—it teaches beauty and grace. To be an actor, and to select your roles on the basis of your heart's desire—this is a service. As you'll find out later in the book, it was because of the movie *Alive* that I was catalyzed to launch the first AIDSRide. To be a schoolteacher, and to have a vision for your teaching—that's a service. Maybe you want to be a kindergarten teacher. Then go be a kindergarten teacher, but be the best kindergarten teacher in the world. Bring a sense of vision, a sense of bigness to your dream, even if your dream seems small to you. Find out what the aptitude scores are in your state for kindergarten teachers, and see if you can't have the highest scores in the state. Teach your students about the world they live in. Give them the spirit of dreaming—then you'll be of service.

The call to parenting is probably one of the most universal and important callings on the planet. My mom's whole life has been about service. Clearly, she understood that part of her calling was to be of service to four children—to help to nurture and support them so that they could live lives of service as well. My mom gave up what might have been her own agenda to pursue this calling.

Gandhi's calling isn't the only kind of call to service. My mom was probably the single greatest reason I was able to pull myself out of the depths of the despair I endured in my 20s, because, no matter how dark the tunnel got, I could always see a ray of light down at the end—which was and is the love for myself that she gave me. My dad did this, too. I had a foundation of love that was so strong that almost no amount of darkness could keep me from returning to it. Sadly, many people don't have that, and they never find their way back to the light. If you didn't have that, it doesn't mean you can't. It just means you have to work to build it for yourself. To do that is to be the greatest kind of hero.

Who are some of the people in your own life who know what to "live about"? What lesson do they teach? What can you learn from them? How can you be inspired and instructed by them?

The call to service can also manifest in ordinary people doing extraordinary things—like any one of the thousands of people who have participated in one of our events. These events, if you haven't already picked up on this, are not easy. They can be extremely demanding. At times, people suffer—climbing the hills, waking up on cold mornings in a tent, weathering wind and rain. The amazing thing is that the people who participate in our events are not athletes or jocks. They're not, by and large, cyclists. Some of them have a bit of a gut, a bit of a butt—some of them have creaky knees, and many of them have lots of gray hair. They're ordinary people who have decided, out of a deep desire to move beyond their limits and to be of service in an extraordinary way, to do something that they would never have thought they were capable of.

They choose to put themselves in demanding circumstances in the name of service, and out of that, they learn incredible things about themselves.

Here are a couple of letters that demonstrate people who know what their lives are about:

"After participating in my fourth AIDS Ride,
I have learned the true meaning of 'I'mpossible.'
I have the power to help . . .
I have the power to encourage . . .
I have the power to support . . .
I have the power to face my own fears . . .
I have the power to speak . . .
I have the power to listen . . .
I have the power to speed things up . . .
I have the power to slow things down . . .
I have the power to teach . . .
I have the power to learn . . .
I have the power to act . . .
But I do not have the power to sit by the wayside . . .
Every year I do the Ride, I can look into the faces of riders and other crew and know that we all have a purpose—to realize what the possibilities are."
— Alisa Curry, RPT, Sports Medicine Crew

"When I signed up for the Ride, I believed I was compelled to do so. I thought about a little girl that I took care of during my pediatrics rotation. 'Karla' was about three years old. She had been abandoned in the hospital. No one visited her, she had no toys tucked around her bed. The only things around her were the medical equipment, the blinking lights of the IV machine, and the beep of the oxygen monitor. Karla was in full-blown AIDS. The other nursing students and I cared for her during our six-week peds rotation. We learned that she never crawled on the floor, never felt the sunlight on her face unless it was filtered through a window. She had never felt a breeze on her face. I knew then why I wanted

to do the ride. I wanted to achieve the I'MPOSSIBLE for her and others like her.

"*I hadn't been on a bike in 20 years. I had over 50 pounds of extra weight, having given birth to twins about a year before. I felt driven to complete the ride and I did. Friends that I met during training said that I was a person driven. 'Are you finished, let's go.' I pushed myself over each hill and thrilled at each downhill.*

"*I cried over the ride. I cried for Karla, I cried for the roads that I covered, I cried for the souls of my ancestors who slaved in the fields. I reached down in myself and found someone that I thought I lost many years ago. I found the courage to face what I was, and look forward to what I would become. I looked toward the hills and knew that I could overcome them.*

"*In the years that have passed since my first ride, I have become a better person. I have been able to teach my children and my parents something about life. My husband has a better wife. I am less than I could be, but more than I was. I don't think about me, I think about others, and I have learned that I am truly blessed.*"

— Trish Chittams

The Call to Kindness

Whether or not our lifetime calling is to be a mother, or an astronaut, or to create great social change, there's another kind of calling—another kind of destiny—that's more about moments, that we can integrate into our lives and that will round out and complete our sense of destiny. That calling is to kindness. Perhaps, in the search for our destiny, the notion that we're meant to be kind to one another is the easiest aspect to arrive at of all. If we never arrive at any other conclusion about our calling in life, the call to kindness is enough. Everyone can make their life, on a daily basis, about being kind to others—and in that sense, no one needs to be left without a sense of their destiny. This is *every* man and woman's destiny.

I want to tell you a story about Alan John Gurd. Alan was an angel who came into my life in October of 1998, and he left in November of 1999. We were boyfriends. Lovers. Best friends. Soulmates. We were meant for each other, and we were a part of one another's destinies.

Alan was the kindest, finest human being I ever met. He had a generosity of spirit that I had never encountered before, nor have I encountered it since. Alan was born in Northern Ireland in 1970, and his family moved to Cleveland in the late '70s. He was as handsome as John Kennedy, and as smart as a Supreme Court justice. He was fun. He was funny. He was a runner, too. In fact, he was one of the fastest runners in the world, finishing the half-mile in Olympic qualifying time. He was 28 years old when I met him—and he was 29 when he died.

Alan would listen to you in a way that I never saw anyone listen before. He didn't care if he got a chance to talk or tell his own story or make his thoughts known—not if there was something important on your mind. He could look deep into a person's soul and know if there was something they were sad or troubled about, even if it wasn't apparent to most other people, or even if they weren't showing it. His insight was that strong—his perception that good. He would seek out people who had something on their mind, or something heavy in their heart, and magically, they would seek him out, too.

On Thanksgiving of 1999, we went home together to visit my family in Boston. Alan, my mom and dad, and I were sitting in the living room one night. My dad started telling Alan that he'd been a runner in high school himself, which I knew. But then my dad started telling him about his specific race times, which, to my astonishment, my dad had remembered. These were his trophies—he didn't have any *actual* trophies, but these *times* were his trophies. They were impressive, even to Alan, and I could tell right then and there that they were precious to my father. Then he started to tell Alan about his training regimen as a kid. He told him about how jogging wasn't something that people really did back in the '50s, and how he used to run in the streets in the wintertime to practice. People would look at him kind of strange because they weren't used to it, and how because there was slush and snow in the streets he used to go running in his boots— which made him look even a little stranger.

I was sitting there watching Alan listen to my dad, and the more he'd listen, the more my dad would tell him, and I was taken aback by it. My dad was revealing very important things about his past, his dreams, his efforts, and his sorrows that I had never known about him. In 38 years, I had never heard these things, and yet Alan, whom my dad had known for less than a year and had spent less than five days with, was drawing all of this stuff out of him. It was because he was listening, and I realized, that in all these years, I had never really listened to my dad—not *really*. I had never listened to him—100 percent—without attention on myself and my own accomplishments, the way Alan was listening to him. I guess I was always so busy trying to impress him that it never dawned on me that my dad might enjoy having someone really listen to *him* just once—really hear his own life story—hear about his own precious dreams. It was Alan's kindness that was making this moment possible.

Who do you have in your life who you can count on to listen to you? What can you learn about listening from them? What kind of listener are you? How present are you when you're listening?

When Alan was younger and living in Cleveland, he used to keep old sweaters that he didn't need in the back seat of his car in case he ever saw a homeless person who might need one. He wasn't embarrassed about doing that. He didn't care how it would look to other people for him to be conversing with a homeless person who might be lonely, cold, and in need of some friendship and a little kindness.

One day, my parents were visiting, and Alan and I took them to Old Town Pasadena to walk around and do a little shopping. We were all in a Crate and Barrel together, and at some point Alan was done looking around and walked outside the store. I bought something and was still in there with my folks. When we walked outside, I couldn't find him—but then I saw him at the crosswalk helping a severely disabled person get across the street. This guy looked like he might be homeless, too. When they got across the street, Alan introduced him to us—his name was Tom. Not only did Alan have the decency to help him across the street, but he had the sensitivity to realize that finding out his name and introducing him to us, like we do with our friends, might be a source of dignity for the guy.

Alan taught me to never hesitate to help someone. He never hesitated. It's in that moment when we hesitate that our minds rationalize us out of helping someone and steal a special moment from us. We see someone broken down in the middle of the street, and the thought absolutely occurs to us to pull over and help, but we hesitate, and in the space of that hesitation, a voice gets in there and says, "Well, I've got to get to this appointment, and someone else will probably help, and I'll just cause more commotion," and on and on, and before we know it, we've been robbed of a beautiful moment to help someone in need. Alan never hesitated, so he never rationalized, and he had a lot of beautiful moments with a lot of people in need.

Alan used to volunteer his time working one-on-one with little kids with AIDS. There was this one little girl he used to visit named LaToya. Her grandmother was her guardian, so Alan would go to the hospital to visit with the two of them; or to take them out for a drive or an ice cream or a hamburger. In fact, on the day that LaToya died, Alan went to visit her, and she wanted to go to a fast-food restaurant to get a hamburger— so Alan took her and her grandmother out to get her favorite food. I can't think of a better way to spend your last few hours than going out with your grandmother and Alan Gurd to get a hamburger and milkshake at a fast-food restaurant. Those were the types of simple, kind gifts that Alan gave to people.

There was an artistry to Alan's kindness, and a power in it. It was the most attractive thing I ever saw. Kindness is a lot more attractive than a great body, lots of accomplishments, or being rich—Alan taught me that it's an essential element of our destinies here, and he kept me from missing out on it in my own life.

Alan died on November 30, 1999. He had just passed the California bar exam—one of the toughest in the nation—on his first try, and he was about to be sworn in as an American citizen, all in the week he died. He was working at one of the most prestigious law firms in Los Angeles, and he absolutely hated the job. He hated the greed of it, and he hated what he was reading about the clients he was going to be asked to defend. Nothing about it suited him—there was nothing he admired about their lives or their behaviors.

The morning that he died, he sent an e-mail to a friend of his who worked at the Elizabeth Glaser Pediatric AIDS Foundation, where he had volunteered for several months while he was studying for the bar. Can you imagine that? He volunteered there while he was in the midst of studying for the most difficult and important exam in his life. In that e-mail, he said he felt lost. The law firm was "hell." Alan felt severed from his calling. A few hours later, he left the office and took his own life. As Don McLean wrote about Vincent Van Gogh's suicide in his song, "Vincent": "This world was never meant for one as beautiful as you." In Alan's case, there were a lot of unfortunate things that had happened to him that left him unable, ultimately, to be kind and patient with the most important person of all—himself. The world lost a great human being on November 30, 1999, and I lost my very best friend in the world. I lost my partner, and I felt as if I'd lost my future as well. The words, "Alan passed away," which his roommate told me over the phone on that terrible night, well, they'll ring a sadness in my ears until the day I die.

After Alan died, I returned to my songwriting, and I actually wrote an entire album of songs about our time together, the lyrics from one of the songs I share with you here. It's about a question I ask myself all the time now in every situation where I have the opportunity to help someone. The question is, "What would Alan do?" Here are the lyrics:

What Alan Would Do

> There was a little girl out on the street today
> With a homemade sign selling lemonade
> It was a busy day I had things to do
> Do I stop to buy or drive on through?
> And a busy world rushes by unmoved
> But I know what Alan would do
> When he was 17 in his back seat
> He saved up sweaters that he didn't need
> And their purpose there was simply won
> If he saw a homeless man who needed one
> It's the kind of thing that humbles you
> Kind of thing Alan would do

There was a migrant man with his little son
On the street last weekend with his
truck broke down
Stacked up high with branches, high with leaves
Replacing brake pads down on their knees
I had sodas in the fridge so I took out two
Thinkin' 'bout what Alan would do.

Alan's death created a resolve in me to carry on the kindness that was so integral to him. And in following the impulse to be kind, I've found a kind of calling that's completely satisfying. If no other dreamy idea ever comes to me, I know I have the ability to be kind to others; and on a case-by-case, moment-to-moment basis, to feel that I'm fulfilling my destiny.

People often come away from Pallotta TeamWorks events saying that they wish they didn't have to leave. They say that it feels like this is the way they wish the world could always be. That's because people are kind to one another—we encourage people to experiment rigorously with their calling to kindness while they're at our events, and they take us up on the invitation, often in very big, very inspiring ways.

The day before each event, every participant is required to watch an hour-long safety and orientation video. This is one of the things we tell people in that video:

"Over the next few days, if you keep your eyes open, you'll see dozens and dozens of opportunities to be kind to people. Try not to hesitate. And try not to be embarrassed. Maybe it's someone having a hard time making it up a hill who needs encouragement. There have been riders in years past who would go up and down the same hill five or six times just so they could cheer on the riders who are having a hard time. Maybe you could do that, even though you know the shower line at camp is going to get a little longer.

"Maybe there's someone who needs help setting up their tent. Or maybe there's someone who doesn't need help setting up their tent. But you offer to help them anyway even though you know the dinner line might be getting longer. Maybe someone has a heavy duffel bag they're trying to drag across camp. No one would expect

you to help out—I mean, you've got your own duffel bag. But it would be a nice surprise. And it would be very sweet. And it might make that person's day. It might even make yours. Maybe you could buy Popsicles at the end of your day and hand them to riders getting in later. See how creative you can be with your kindness.

"Over the next few days, be kind to yourself, and look for ways to be kind to others. That's what we built the AIDSRide for. So people would have a chance to live in a world, at least for a few days, that is the way they always wished the world could be. So that people could leave their old identities behind them, and create a great work of art with their little acts of kindness."

I had a rider come up to me on this year's Boston-New York AIDSRide, and he said that he had fixed eleven flats on that ride. And he said, "None of them were my own." I have to tell you, when I think about this grand concept of changing the world, I don't think about the policy changes and other things that presidential candidates talk about in their campaigns. I think about people fixing flat tires that are not their own. I think about people pulling off the side of the road to help a broken-down motorist in need. And in that sense, it is everyone's destiny to change the world.

I believe the reason that people are so attracted to Pallotta TeamWorks' events, and the reason they get kind of depressed when the events are over, is because for a few days, they have been put in touch with a part of their real calling in life, and they've been hungry for it for years.

Have you ever noticed, how, in a situation of great crisis, people become naturally kind to one another? I remember the blizzard of 1978 in Boston. The streets were closed to traffic statewide by the governor, so people were going around with snowmobiles and sleds buying groceries for the elderly, and helping one another. In fact, helping other people became the *most* important thing—they were actually hungry for opportunities to help someone— they were hunting for them, the way we usually hunt for ways to get ahead, and were visibly disappointed when they couldn't find anyone to help.

During the Northridge earthquake in Los Angeles in 1994—which I was right in the middle of—all of a sudden, people who never even talked to one another before were offering to share batteries when the store was running out, and they loved it. It was because they were being returned to their true selves—to their destinies.

In the last few days, when did you hesitate when there was a chance to be kind? Were there any homeless people who asked you for help? Did you help? If not, did you have an impulse to? What stopped you? Were you afraid of being conned? Were you afraid of what someone might think if they saw you? Were you with friends? Were you afraid of what they would have thought? What few things could you do tomorrow to be kind? Who has done something kind for you recently? Have you done anything kind for yourself recently?

Be Kind to Yourself

You have a calling. You have a destiny. You may understand it or you may not—you may understand it one moment and lose it in another. It's made up of your own unique passions, abilities, and desires, and it's made up of an innate desire to make a difference in the world, to make the world a better place, and to be kind to other people. It needs only to be uncovered. If you'll open yourself up to it, and follow it, your moments will come, and your life will define itself. But be kind to yourself—don't go out there devising schemes and concocting dreams that have no basis in what you want your life to be about. Develop an understanding of what it is that you stand for in life so that you won't be battered about by the rat race that tells you have to accomplish, accomplish, accomplish all in the name of accomplishment itself.

Your happiness lies in discovering that special, unique destiny that is your very own, which doesn't look like anyone else's. Your destiny doesn't have to be big or complicated. Give yourself a break—you bought a book about dreams, and that book is telling you *not* to try to come up with a dream. Let go of the pressure to follow your dream, and begin a search for yourself and your purpose here. The dreams will come, effortlessly, out of that knowledge.

Last, calling isn't limited to one thing, and it doesn't occur just once. It occurs constantly and is ongoing. The question *What is my life about?* is one that it would serve all of us to ask ourselves with tremendous frequency. Let the answer to that question guide you in all things, and keep it close by your side all your life. The question, not the answer, is the thing that has real value. Live the question, and the answers will manifest naturally and effortlessly.

Chapter Four

Allowing Your Dreams to Come to You

Chris's Story

My sister Nancy and her husband, Cecil, have two beautiful children, Christopher and Jessica. Chris is ten and Jessica is eight. Back in the summer of 1997, Chris had a fever that wouldn't go away. It lasted more than a week. Then it went into its second week, and my sister was nervous. She'd been to the doctor with Chris, but the doctor couldn't find anything wrong. Then Chris began complaining of pain in his bones, so the doctor ordered a CAT scan. My mom called me and said that they found small tumors all over Chris's body and that he had leukemia. We were all scared to death. Chris is the oldest of my parents' grandchildren, and he's a precious kid with a great smile and great character, which is a rare thing to see developing in any kid.

I flew back to Boston, went to FAO Schwarz, and bought a couple of bags full of toys. I went over to Children's Hospital in Boston, where Chris was being cared for, and went into his room with just one of the toys. He was really glad to see me, and he was happy that I brought him a toy. I love to play around with him. I said, "Oh, wait a minute, wait a minute—I think I forgot something," and I went out into the lobby and got another toy out of the bag. He laughed. Then I did it again with another toy, and with another until all ten or twelve of the toys were gone. That got him laughing pretty hard.

His dad was there with him, and he looked really sad. And my sister was beside herself. They were doing all kinds of very painful tests on Chris, and every time they came in to get him for another one, it just broke his parents' hearts. He'd start scream- ing, "Daddy, Daddy, don't let them, please don't let them," and Cecil was just torn apart because he wanted to protect Chris so badly, but there was nothing he or my sister could do. There were lots of needles, and then those very painful lumbar extractions or whatever you call them. It was horrible.

The nurses at Children's Hospital were good to Chris, and they made a big difference in helping my sister feel more at ease. Of course, every once in a while there was one who had the oppo- site effect, but overall, Nancy was really taken with the level of care and compassion they offered.

Thankfully, the prognosis for Chris was good. There's a high rate of cure in childhood leukemia now something like in excess of 90 percent of kids with leukemia get cured—and Christopher responded well to the chemotherapy. He lost his hair and all, but the doctors seem to have saved his life.

In the last year, Nancy, who never really liked school, has gone back so she can become a nurse. She's taking courses in anatomy and chemistry as I write, and was just accepted into a very prestigious nursing school for the second part of her train- ing. She's 38 years old, married, has two kids, and her moment has come.

She watched the nurses that took care of Chris, and it inspired her to want to do the same thing. Had Chris not been diagnosed with leukemia, she might never have taken this path. It's an amazing example of how the ideas come when they've a mind to. Part of Nancy's calling was to be a mother, and she's a wonderful mom. But I think she always had the intention of doing something with her life in addition to being a mother—something that would make a difference even beyond her family. Had Nancy spent a lot of time trying and struggling to figure out what that was, it would have probably all been for naught. As it turned out, there was no need for struggle, no need for effort or frustration. Her destiny showed up on her doorstep. The universe could plainly see that her life was about children, and it could see that she wanted to be handed more of her life—and that's exactly what it did for her.

As Victor Hugo once said, "There is nothing more powerful than an idea whose time has come." Once you have a sense of your calling, how do you come up with the ideas to fulfill that calling? Where do they come from? Every dream I ever pursued came to me when I wasn't trying to find it—conversely, whenever I was trying to find a dream, it wouldn't come. So stop banging your head against the wall trying to figure out what you're supposed to do. Just because you may understand your calling doesn't mean you're called on constantly. John Denver said that "the songs come when they've a mind to," and the same thing goes for ideas. They come when they've a mind to, and not a moment before—there's nothing you can do to speed them up or slow them down. An idea will come when it's time has come.

A famous songwriter was being interviewed by Charlie Rose one night, and he was asked how often he writes. His response was: "When I have an idea." This should be your approach to dreams as well. I used to try to write songs without an idea, and I failed miserably. When the time came that I finally had an idea, the songs wrote themselves. Develop your dreams when you have an idea, and don't develop them when you don't.

Go to the Beach

I remember that back in 1982, I wanted to have a really relaxing summer, so I decided to buy a bike as a gift to myself. There were some nice tree-covered roads around our house in Melrose, and I was sort of just looking forward to riding them in the early evenings after I finished my work doing maintenance at the Breakhart Lake Reservation not far from our house. I bought a really nice maroon Schwinn ten-speed. I really liked it, and I did do a lot of bike riding that summer. I was being kind to myself.

There's a long, narrow beach about six miles north of where we lived called Nahant. I loved that place, and started riding out there once in a while that summer. I'd purchased a Sears transistor radio that mounted onto the handlebars of my bike, and after I packed up from the beach and headed home, I turned it on. A news story came on about these two guys from the Boston area who had just completed a bike ride across America for the benefit of a Jimmy Fund—a well-known cancer research effort in Boston that the Red Sox supported that helped kids with childhood leukemia. I never found out who these two people were, and they may never know what their courageous journey wrought. Whoever they are, I owe them a huge debt of gratitude.

The minute I heard the news story, I had a sense that my moment had come. A bike ride across America. A bike ride across the whole damned continent. It's epic. It's impossible. It's bold. This is it. This is the idea I've been waiting for. You just know. There's no doubt. If anything, there's a kind of fear, because you know you're going to be swept away to your destiny, and you know you're going to a new place. The fear is a pretty good sign that you've encountered an idea whose time has come.

I had about five miles left to go at this point to get back home. It literally felt as if this idea had dropped into my lap. As soon as the "light-bulb went on," I rushed home—it was like Charlie from *Willie Wonka and the Chocolate Factory* in that scene where he's just opened the chocolate bar and found the last remaining golden ticket—he rushes home in, like four-minute mile time, knowing his moment had come—he couldn't wait to get there and tell his mom and his grandparents that he was going to see the inside of the mysterious Wonka chocolate works. I felt like that.

Every second, the idea was generating more energy. I started to think about how many people would need to be involved. *Two? Five? Ten? Twenty? More? Yes, more. We should have 40 or 50 people. We'll recruit students at school. What will we need? Trucks? Vans? What should the route be?*

How will we get there? How will we eat? Where will we stay? How will it raise money? How are we going to train? What should the logo look like? What are we going to call it? Where do I start? Ideas whose time have come race at you with the force of a comet. They come at light speed—they come with so much excitement and energy that they sweep you off your feet. They do if you embrace them. If you turn away from them, they die.

As I said earlier, my friend Mark Takano and I started planning the project as soon as we got back to school, and you know the rest of the story. But it's a clear example of an idea coming in its own good time. There would have been little I could have done to make it come any sooner. In fact, had I tried to contrive another idea, I might have been too busy working on something that was ill-conceived, and I might have been doing something else that day instead of taking a relaxing ride to the beach. I would never have heard that radio story. I never would have been relaxed enough to let the idea for Ride for Life come my way. What's important is that you have the intention to make good on your destiny. If you truly have the intention, the ideas will come your way.

What ideas have fallen into your lap? What great ideas have you carried around with you for a long time? What do you do with them? Do you ever force ideas, poems, songs, or other things to come to you? How does that feel? What ideas have you had that were discouraged by someone? Did you give them up? Why? If not, what happened? When did you sense that "this is my moment"?

Letting the Love of Your Life Come Your Way

One of the dreams that people often try to force has to do with their love lives. I realize that this may seem a little outside of the realm of what we're discussing here, but love is a dream, isn't it? How do we make it come true? Well, like the other ideas we're discussing here, we have to relax and let go of the strategies we've designed to "make" it happen.

Have you ever seen those "Where's Waldo?" puzzles? They're these busy puzzles with lots of people and things in them, and somewhere in each puzzle is this character named Waldo. Waldo wears blue pants, a red-and-white striped shirt, and glasses and some funky hat; he's always in the middle of a big, crowded scene, and you're supposed to find him.

This is how a lot of people approach the great love of their lives—like they have to go out and find him or her in the midst of a very busy world, and that the responsibility rests entirely on their shoulders. They feel they have to work very hard and try every angle, nook, and cranny to locate this person. There's an almost total lack of faith in the idea that God will help you and your love find one another. My therapist, Kris, always said to me with respect to relationships that if you're meant to be together, wild horses couldn't keep you apart—and if you're not, wild horses couldn't pull you together.

There was a period in my life when I was driving myself crazy trying to find my own Waldo. I remember going to the Gay Pride festival in Los Angeles every summer, where there were in excess of 100,000 eligible men, and I hated it. I was so exhausted by the time the day was over that I needed a vacation. Why? Because I was constantly strategizing, trying to be in the right place at the right time, just in case Mr. Perfect—whoever he was—was there. If I was over by the hot dog stand, I'd be concerned that maybe Waldo was actually by the stage, and if I was at the stage, I was worried that Waldo might be over on the other side of the festival.

It's a big world out there. Trying to always be at the right place at the right time, at the right party, or the right club on the right night, can be pretty tiring. In a world of nearly six billion people, trying to find the right person without any help from God or the universe is pretty ridiculous.

I remember a woman who's struggled with the same obsessive issues that I do telling me one day: "I'm just so ready to love someone." I told her she should be careful of that—how can you be so ready to love someone whom you haven't even met? The person should come first, and *then* the love, not the other way around. But I think that a lot of people get into bad relationships, pursuing people who just aren't treating them well or aren't right for them, simply because they're "so ready to love someone"—because they want it so badly. They shouldn't be ready to love just anyone. It's hard to find the right person. *But it's easy to let the right person come to you.* Just like it's easy to let the ideas come to you. It may take a long, long time, but in the end, that's why you'll call them special. You don't call things that you see all over the place special. You use that word for the things that are rare to you. That's what *special* means.

Fortunately, I gave up on trying to find Waldo, and instead, put my faith in God. I decided that if I was meant to be with someone, there would be no avoiding that person. About a year after that decision, my friend Loren called me up. He said that his niece, Diana, whom I'd really only met three or four times, had a friend at law school who had broken up with someone about six months earlier—she thought we'd be perfect for each other, and she wanted to give him my phone number. I said, "Sure."

Loren called me back about three days before Halloween in 1998 and said, "Okay, you're going to be getting a call from a guy named Alan Gurd, so be expecting it." I didn't think too much of it, but a few days later, Alan left me a message. I can still remember how much I liked the sound of his voice that first time on my answering machine. We spoke over the phone, and he sounded really bright and funny—I liked that, and we made plans to have dinner. The moment Alan walked into the restaurant, I knew it was *him*, before he even introduced himself, and before our dinner was over, I had a calm sense of knowing that the two of us would probably have a wonderful life together. It wasn't an adrenaline rush—it was just a knowing, and it felt right. Not crazy. Just right. You know how some people say they just *fell* in love? You know how some people say they're *crazy* over someone? I don't know about you, but I don't want to be falling and crazy. I want to be standing and calm. That's how I felt after an evening with Alan.

What's interesting here is that about a month before, I'd met someone who was really gorgeous and sexy, and he triggered a lot of my attraction buttons. But he was clearly ambiguous about whether or not he wanted a long-term relationship. This raised a red flag for me, because I knew that I *did* want a lifelong partner. It was important to me, and I wanted to be with someone who shared that vision of a lasting, monogamous relationship.

In the past, I might have conveniently overlooked everything he was telling me, let my own self-willed desire to fulfill my attraction to him take over, and gotten myself into a dating situation with someone who I knew was wrong for me from the very start. But this time, I saw the red flag and I heeded it, and I said no to even one more date with this guy. It was a statement of my intent—a statement to the universe that I was ready to face my real life—not my fantasy life, and that I was ready to have my dreams. That's kind of what this whole book is about. That's what that moment in my life was about. I was finally ready for the right person to enter my life.

To me, the way that Alan came into my life underscores everything I want to say about the idea of "letting" the love of your life, and the ideas of your life, come to you—without forcing them, scheming them, or strategizing. I had the hope of a loving relationship in my heart for a long time. I was frightened it might never come true, and I had no idea who that special person would or should be. Alan didn't come when I wanted him to, but when he did, he was right on time

Finally, an Album

For years, I tried to get a recording contract. I love the sound of an acoustic guitar, and I love to sing and I love to play. But the desire to get a record deal was misguided. I would try to write songs without any idea what I wanted to write about. I would copy this or that artist to try to make my records sound commercial, but there was no originality. Still, there was this honest love of music—that was genuine. There was an intention, somewhere deep in me, that wanted to express something real one day through music. In fact, once in a while, after Pallotta TeamWorks was well on its way, I would talk to Bryn Mathieu, who had produced most of my demos; and Rob Allen, who had played guitar on most of them, and muse about one day taking six months off of work to write a country music album with them. Sometimes, just like in that case, ideas whose times *will* come peek out at you years before they're actually ready to come.

On Christmas Day of 1999, 25 days after Alan died, I was sitting in the spare bedroom in my house where I have my guitars and some of my sound equipment. My parents and my siblings and some of my friends had given me Christmas presents, and I went in the spare bedroom with some orange juice, put on a tape of music that Alan had made me, and began to open my presents. I was so sad. I couldn't stop crying. Every lyric and every note reminded me of him. And there were no Christmas presents for Alan or from him . . . or so I thought.

There was one song in particular that Alan loved called "Could Not Ask for More." I started thinking that it had been a long time since I learned a song, and that I'd like to learn that one. I found myself wishing that I'd learned it a long time ago so I could have played it for Alan. I picked up my guitar, figured out the chords, wrote down the lyrics, and learned to play it. Then I started playing around with other chords on the guitar, and something new happened—an idea for a song began to come to me.

The idea for the song centered around a question. I was wondering where, in the great expanse of the cosmos, Alan had gone. Was there anyplace I could go to find him? If I searched the farthest galaxy, would he be there? There's a deep crevice on the moon, about a mile deep and 15 miles long, called Hadley Rille, which was explored by the Apollo 15 astronauts. I started to write a song about Hadley Rille. It was a question: "Up on Hadley Rille, in some crater on the moon, if I went up there, is that where I'd find you? Or infinity—on some outpost galaxy, if I took a ship out there, is that where you'd be? Is that where you'd be?"

Once I had the idea for "Hadley Rille," I went out into the kitchen with my journal, and in about 20 minutes, with only a couple of phrases scratched out, I wrote all the lyrics to the song. It used to take me weeks to write a song, and there would be pages and pages filled with potential lyrics. Clearly, something new was happening. I thought to myself how cool it was that I'd written a song in tribute to Alan. What a beautiful memorial—I hadn't written a song in about eight years. It was still Christmas Day.

I felt another song coming on. *Two?* I thought. *Could I actually have two songs in me about Alan?* The second song was written the same day, and it was called "Run No More." There were only three phrases crossed out and replaced. Then a third song started coming to me, entitled "A Sad Sohn." Alan, because he still had traces of his Irish accent, never pronounced the "G" at the end of a word that ended in "ng." For instance, "strong," was pronounced "stronh," and "song" was pronounced "sohn," so "A Sad Sohn" is a tribute to his accent.

Within the next week, before New Year's Eve, I had written "Still Believe" and "A Prayer for Alan Gurd"—five new songs in all. On New Year's Eve, I went out to Zuma Beach—I'd heard that when a friend of Alan's died of cancer, he let a white balloon go up into the sky at the beach for her. After our second week together, Alan brought over two roses—one for each week. So I bought two roses and two white balloons and went to Zuma. I let the balloons go, cast the roses into the sea, and then lay down on the beach and looked up at the stars for a while, wondering if Alan was up there somewhere. I actually caught a satellite out of the corner of my eye and watched it travel across the sky. On the way home, I wrote another song in my head, which was unusual—I usually need my guitar to write. It was called "Two Roses." The next day, I wrote "Hypocrisy." Eight songs. I felt I had enough to actually record an album.

But the songs kept coming. There was nothing I could do about it. I was a channel for all these ideas, and they wanted to be written. Over the next few weeks, I wrote "Anthem," "The Gift," "Spirit," "Everybody Wants a Friend," "The Truth," "What Alan Would Do," "Reunion," "Spirit of the Dead," and "Lonesome Coyote." Seventeen songs. Can you imagine that? Now we had more songs than we could fit on one album. I was going to have to start cutting songs off the record. Three more songs came—"Lost People," "Candlelight," and "Dark Angels." They were just going to have to wait for a second album. I had 20 songs in all—and every single one of them was better than anything I'd ever written when I was trying so hard. Every one of them was more honest, more solid, more lyrical, and more beautiful.

I decided I wanted to do them more justice than just a simple demo-type of recording. Bryn and I started working on a real, honest-to-goodness album. I played all of the acoustic guitars, but Rob Allen added some beautiful baritone guitar, and we had other musicians play harmonica and keyboards. The album was just about complete, and we were ready to go to print with the liner notes, but I wasn't sure which song I wanted for the title song. It was a toss-up between "Spirit" and "The Gift," but I didn't want to struggle over the decision.

I was out for a run one morning, and I offered a prayer up to Alan. I said that whichever word I saw first—*spirit* or *gift*—would be the title of the album. On my way home, I saw a white Volvo go by. Its license plate said, simply, "TSAGIFT," in other words, "'tis a gift." Not only did I have 20 songs that came without effort, I had a title, too.

I sent the album out to hundreds of friends who had supported me through the difficult months since Alan's death. (It's available for sale on our Website: **www.pallottateamworks.com.**)

The story of "The Gift" demonstrates, better than anything else I could say, the simple truth that you have no control over when the ideas come. They come when they want to, so there's nothing to fret about. You don't have to move through the process with a stopwatch. Keep your intention alive. Keep playing at life 100 percent. The universe will not let you down. The ideas may not come when you want them to, but when they do, they'll be right on time.

Is there a dream you've been unable to make happen? Does it feel like it is or isn't meant to be? What things have come easily to you when you weren't even looking?

This Book

Sometimes—and this is important—ideas come to you that you never even asked for. I never had a big dream, or even a little dream, of writing a book. I certainly never had a dream of getting a book that I'd written published. So you see, to start out with a dream that you want to write a book, without any idea of your calling, or any idea of what the book should be about, would be doing it backwards. If you're truly in touch with your calling, you'll become a channel for dreams and ideas that are consistent with that calling, even though you may not have been asking for them.

Abraham Lincoln didn't ask to be the person who had to guide the nation through the Civil War, but he accepted that responsibility as part of his calling. In fact, these ideas—the ones you weren't even asking for— are probably the most life-defining of them all, because they came to you from a context of complete detachment—not a *moment* of it, but a *context* of it. In other words, when I relaxed enough one summer to buy a bicycle and have some fun and the Ride for Life idea came to me, that was a summer of—and a moment of—detachment. But the context was that I wanted an idea that would allow me to do something about hunger. This book, on the other hand, came to me when I wasn't looking for an idea at all, so it has a purity that makes it particularly of my calling, with no influence from me added.

Big Sky Dad

So many of us, myself included, fret about our lives passing us by. We worry and wonder when we're going to make our mark, when, in reality, we have absolutely no control over it. Some people don't make their mark until they're 50, 60, 70, 80, or even 90. You never know when your moments are going to come, and if they don't come until we're 70 years old, that's okay. Remember "Granny D" Haddock, the 90-year-old woman who walked clear across America? Look at when one of *her* moments came.

My parents have attended many of our events. They've been to many of the opening and closing ceremonies. They were on the volunteer crew for the very first California AIDSRide serving lunches for seven days; my mom and two sisters walked in the Boston Breast Cancer 3-Day, and my dad served on the lunch crew for that event. But after I returned from my Alaska Ride in August of 2000, I sent all my friends and family the same journal entry that I shared with you in Chapter 1. There was something about those words that gave my dad an idea, which brought him one of his moments. He called me and said that he was going to do the Montana AIDS Vaccine Ride with me in July of 2001, over his 66th birthday weekend.

I have to tell you that I'm more than a little cautious for him. The Montana Ride will be one of our most demanding: It's seven days long, goes right smack through the Rocky Mountains, and crosses the Continental Divide at over 6,000 feet, where the hills will be tough and the oxygen will be in short supply. Bear in mind that my dad, while in good health, hasn't been on a bike in probably 40 years, and he's not actively athletic. When he called, I said to him, "I'll tell you what—why don't I talk to our logistics people and see just how tough the hills are going to be, and if it looks like they're going to be too hard, we'll do the shorter Vaccine Ride from Montreal to Maine instead." His response was inspiring, and it demonstrated that he was in the fire of his own moment. He said, simply, "No, I made up my mind. I'm going to do Montana."

When the Montana Ride is over, I know that my dad will feel, if he never does another altruistic thing in his life, that he's fulfilled his desire to make a difference in the world, and that sense of fulfillment will be completely without doubt. The lesson is that the fulfillment comes in its own sweet time.

Has your desire to make a difference ever been fulfilled? Would you climb the Continental Divide to fulfill it? If not, why? If yes, how do you think you'll feel when you cross over the top? How would it feel to you to look over your shoulder at the Rocky Mountains, knowing that you've crossed them?

How Do You Know If It's Your Moment?

There's a concurrent experience of excitement and dread. There's a sense that your life is about to change in a significant way—a sense that you're about to be lifted. It's like going to the edge of a diving board for the first time—no more difficult than that. You just keep walking toward your destiny. It's a feeling very different from any other kind of feeling in life. You just know. There's no confusion or lack of clarity. Fear, yes, but not confusion. You won't be in two minds about whether or not this is something you're supposed to do.

I've gone skydiving twice. The very first time, as I was at the door of the plane—well, actually, there was no door—with the wind whipping by at 200 miles an hour, 12,000 feet up in the air, I was filled with a simple sense of, "Oh my God, I'm actually going to do this. I'm actually going to walk into a dimension that's going to alter my life forever." That's what it feels like when your moment comes. It's an invitation into a new you. It's an invitation into the next chapter in your life. A new predictor of your potential. It's an invitation into your destiny.

For me, there's always an internal image of something taking flight—or of flying itself. I describe the idea to myself as "having wings." For me, that means that I know the idea wants to fly, and I have a deep, very clear, inner knowing that it *will* fly. I know that the journey will be interesting, demanding, scary, and life-altering, but if I continue to walk toward it, it *will* happen. That's what gives it a sense of destiny. I'm not manufacturing the feeling of destiny. That is, in large part, why it's frightening and exciting—because it's of God—it's of that awesome power. When I see my destiny, it's as if I'm touching the hand of God. I'm not visualizing that destiny—I'm *seeing* it. It's already there. There's a big difference between visualizing and seeing. Visualization requires manufacturing—a destiny can be seen without manufacturing an image. This is a vital distinction. If you can't see something, then it's not there. If you *can* see it, you don't have to visualize it.

I've never given birth to another human being, but I *have* given birth to ideas. And they've given birth to me. It's the most beautiful feeling I know. They sweep you up and take you on to the next level of your life, where you'll see new things, face new fears, encounter new challenges, know new impossibilities, and realize a whole new you. New impossibilities are the most wonderful things in the world. When we launched the very first California AIDSRide in 1994, our goal was to raise a million dollars. That seemed utterly impossible. But in the year 2000, we grossed more than $100 million. A million-dollar goal is now a piece of cake for us—there's absolutely nothing impossible about it. Now, a *billion* dollars feels impossible. I've grown. I have a new impossibility to confront. If we're truly dreaming creatures, then the most meaningful kind of human existence is to continue exploring the impossible frontier, and, in that, to continue exploring and giving birth to ourselves. If a moment comes to you that feels like it's going to do that, then you know that your moment has come.

There's a scene in *Oh God,* that movie that came out around 1980 about God coming down—in the form of George Burns—to get John Denver's character to deliver "His" message of salvation to the world. The two of them have been hanging out for a while, and John Denver says that nobody will believe him if he goes around telling people he's seen God. George Burns says to him, "You have the strength that comes from knowing." That is very much the feeling I have when I encounter an idea whose time has come. I have a knowing. It's mystic.

What one great thing have you always wanted to do? If you proceed with it, do you think it would frighten you? What have you done in your life that, at some point, gave you a sensation of both excitement and dread? Have you felt this sense of knowing I described in your life?

Where We're Going from Here

Identifying your calling and allowing the ideas to come to you requires that you support yourself. It requires that you love yourself instead of pressure yourself. That's what the first chapters of this book have been about. The second part of this book is about courage. Yes, you have to love yourself enough to take the pressure off and let your moments come to you. But when they do, you have to have the courage to pursue them and see them through.

Your moments will come. But there's absolutely no guarantee whatsoever that your moments will materialize. Your moment can come and pass you right by—and fast, if you don't engage it. What happens after the moment arrives is entirely up to you. You can be up in the airplane with your goggles and your parachute on, ready to step out of the open door with a sense that your life is about to change. But you have to step out of the opening. *You* have to do it. *Your path will be shown to you, but only you can walk it.* That's not something God is going to do for you. The first part of this book was about understanding that you were supposed to go skydiving. The second part, upon which we are now embarking, is about stepping out of the door. Both parts are critical to the realization of your destiny and your dreams.

Let's examine the things that will attempt to get in the way once you have a clear sense of what your life is about, and once you've been visited by an idea, dream, or moment whose time has come. We're going to explore four realms. First, the realm of cynicism, which is at play constantly whenever you're doing the work of realizing your dreams. Next, ambiguity, and its opposite, the little-understood realm of commitment. We'll look at how critical commitments are to making your ideas reality. Stepping out of the door of the plane is a statement of your commitment.

After that we're going to examine obstacles and how to interact with them. Finally, we'll take a look at the desire to quit. Each of these things is like a demon in a gauntlet, attempting to keep your dream from becoming a reality. Cynicism, lack of commitment, obstacles, and the desire to quit are four snakes in the garden of Eden—all offering you a tasty apple.

Cynicism says, "You'll never be able to make this happen. Come on, take the apple—it will be much easier if you realize your dream is stupid right at the outset." Ambiguity says, "Oh, just play it by ear—just see how it goes, see how you feel—don't go making any promises. Come on, take the apple. Why pressure yourself with a promise?" Obstacle says, "Well, you can't get around this one. This is impossible. Come on, take the apple—this wall is just too big to breach." And, finally, the desire to quit says, "Quit. Come on, just quit. Take it easy. Take the apple and give this whole thing up." It will be way easier. Yes it will, but that's not what we're here for.

We'll begin the next chapter with cynicism.

PART II
THE BUILDING

Chapter Five
The Trap of Cynicism

Wayne's Story

Whenever you hear the word *cynic*, you usually think it refers to someone else, but we all have cynical voices inside of us. Recognize when you're about to succumb to the chatter of those voices, and don't do it. They're poison, and they could have kept me from meeting this incredible guy named Wayne....

This past summer, I was flying back to Los Angeles from London, with a stopover in Chicago. I was at London's Heathrow Airport, and I had a couple of hours before my seven-hour flight to Chicago. I wasn't that distraught about the long flight ahead of me because I had used frequent-flyer miles to upgrade to a business-class seat.

I'm standing near the departure lounge for my flight—two hours early—and this little old guy comes walking up. He was probably about 70 years old, wearing khaki pants, those cream-colored shoes that a lot of senior citizens wear for walking, a plaid beret, and a tan "Members Only"-type jacket. He was very adorable-looking, actually. He also had a little old suitcase—about two feet wide and a foot high, with a plastic handle. He was roaming around the departure area, and looked as if he'd like to talk, so I said, "Hello."

He asked me if I knew where there was a coffee shop, and I said that I really didn't. So he looked around and didn't see one within close distance. He decided he'd take a walk to try to find one. He asked me if I thought he had time. We had two whole hours. So I nicely said that I thought he probably did, and that I wouldn't let the plane leave without him. I found out that his name was Wayne.

After Wayne returned, they let us sit in the departure lounge. I started talking to him and listening to him, like Alan used to listen to people. He told me about his kids and about his life as an engineer. Apparently his reason for being in London had to do with something very, very secret, as he described it, which I thought was really cute and funny, and I didn't probe him any further. It was "classified information," so I respected that, although I have to say that it seemed like he was really itching to tell me whatever it was that was so secret.

Now for several years, I've had this idea. When I fly, I usually sit in business class. I watch all the other people file onto the plane, and it's sort of like a Norman Rockwell parade of people. I'm particularly struck by the older people, whose faces and hands and clothing seem to tell me that they've worked hard all their lives and that they don't have a lot of money. They always seem very vulnerable and a little scared getting on the plane—worried about the flying, worried about where they'll put their bags—worried if they'll fit in the overheads, and all that. I watch them come in, and I say to myself, "Someday, when I see the right person—who looks just so—who looks like they've had a hard life—I'm going to ask them if they'd like to sit in my business-class seat, so at least once in their lives they won't feel second class— at least once in their lives they'll be treated to the linens on the tray, and the fine service and plush treatment that they deserve."

So I'm sitting there looking at Wayne talking to me, and a voice in my head says, "This is the guy—this is the guy to give your business-class seat to." Then, another much more cynical voice in my head popped up and said, "Come on now, let's be reasonable—let's be practical about this—this is no time to be a nice guy—this is a seven-hour flight. Are you crazy? This is your vacation. You earned this seat. Give up your seat on a shorter flight—not on a seven-hour Atlantic crossing. Come on now, just forget about this—really. You're going to be miserable back there in coach. Don't do it."

While these two voices were at work in my head, I asked Wayne if he'd ever sat in business or first class before, and he said no. I felt a clear sense that one of my moments had come. I thought to myself, *Geez, I think I'm really going to end up doing this.* I had a kind of internal knowing about it, which is always there when it's an idea whose time has come. There's a sort of inevitability to it, and all you have to do is play out your role. I asked myself what Alan would do, and the answer was clear to me. But I wasn't as saintly as that. I said to myself, "Okay, let's see his ticket—if he has an aisle seat in coach, at least I'll be able to stretch my legs out. I hate those middle seats. I get claustrophobic. If he has an aisle seat, I'll do it." So he said he was in 25G— an aisle seat. I went up to the front desk, and asked the ticket agent if I could switch seats with Wayne. I told her he was a guy who'd never sat in business class in all his life, and I wanted to do something nice for him. I asked if she could transfer my business-class seat to his name so he wouldn't get booted out when they found him sitting there.

She looked at me, and after a long pause, said, "Wait a minute . . . I'll tell you what. How'd you *both* like to sit in business class? Here are two seats in business class next to one another. Enjoy your flight. I have to tell you that in 11 years working this desk, I've never once seen anyone do this. It's very nice of you. So I want you both to sit in business class."

So Wayne and I sat in business class the whole way back. I told him about Alan, and he told me about his wife and a woman he loved who recently died of breast cancer. And he told me about his work and his life. I showed him how to use the little personal video player so he got to watch movies, and he was treated to linens and silverware and a nice meal and dessert, and extended leg rests, and all the other amenities of business class.

When I went up to him and told him he was going to get to sit in business class, you should have seen his face. It was like it was the nicest thing anyone had ever done for him. It made me cry inside, and it felt incredibly fulfilling. I felt, once again, that I was living out my true calling. *When I make my calling kindness, it's not very difficult to find at all.*

I also learned from that incident that the universe doesn't want us to be martyrs. The universe stands for bounty. It's not either/or. The universe doesn't say, "Either he sits in business class or you do, but one of you has to suffer a bit." The universe isn't cynical that way. It clearly wanted both of us to sit in business class. I actually think that God wants to put everyone in business class. In fact, I think He wants us all in first class.

"**Cynic:** *A person disposed to rail or find fault; now usually: One who shows a disposition to disbelieve in the sincerity or goodness of human motives and actions, and is wont to express this by sneers and sarcasms; a sneering fault-finder.*"

— Oxford English Dictionary, 1999

The earth is flat. No one will ever run a four-minute mile. Slavery is a fact of life. The sun revolves around the earth. A man on the moon is a pipe dream. These were not the opinions of cynics; these were facts. Cynicism masks itself as truth, crushing dreams and suffocating imagination in its wake. *There will never be a cure for polio. Human beings will never fly. The stock market will never go above 1,000.* Facts. *No one will ever want to watch a 90-minute animated cartoon. Cartoons are supposed to be five minutes long because that's how long they always have been.* "American Pie" is a nine-minute song. *Radio won't play songs longer than three and a half minutes.*

These were things that the cynics "knew," and anyone who challenged them was laughed at as naive, impractical, and foolish. The cynics, you see, are never naive, impractical, or foolish. They're guided by accepted norms.

They conform. Their lives and their opinions can be predicted. They take no risks. They never walk close to the edge. They don't buy books like this. They walk on the side of the trail closest to the mountain.

Today the cynics have different facts—new things they "know." *Humans have always fought one another in wars and they always will—you can never end war. Hunger is a basic fact of life—there will always be people who are hungry. True love is a pipe dream—relationships don't really last, and if they do, it's because you both settle for some compromised version of love. Gay relationships don't last. Crime is a basic fact of life. There's no life on other planets. No human being will ever travel close to the speed of light.* And to see the power of cynicism, notice how you and I don't regard these ideas as opinions. We regard them as facts.

Part of the reason you don't pursue your dreams is because you have facts to back up the obstacles. You don't have an "opinion" that you could never become president of the United States. You "know" it. Come on—you know that, right? You know you could never be president, don't you?

John Kennedy once said, "The problems of the world cannot possibly be solved by the skeptics or the cynics, whose horizons are limited by the obvious realities. We need people who dream of things that never were." Let's break that down.

"The problems of the world cannot be solved by the skeptics or the cynics." Kennedy defied all the odds to become president of the United States. He was the youngest president ever elected—during a time when it was "known" that no Catholic could be elected president of this country. So here's a person with some experience in the arena of achieving dreams, telling us that the skeptics and the cynics aren't the ones who will be leading us into the future. He's telling us that they lack the basic skill-set to solve the problems of the world. Yet we continue to be guided by cynics and skeptics.

"Whose horizons are limited by the obvious realities." All cynics can see is what's real already. They can't see things that aren't *yet* real. They only believe in the obvious, not in that which isn't. The dictionary definition of *dream* is: "To fall into reverie; to indulge in fancies or daydreams; to form imaginary visions of (unrealities)." So cynics can't see a world without hunger; they can't see you completely changing your career; and if you asked them, they would tell you that you're foolish, ridiculous, and

naive beyond words. They would dismiss you. And many of the people who would do this would have impressive resumés and credentials—they're often experts. Professors. Teachers. Captains of business.

Cynics don't attempt to visualize a great dream coming true. They're also unable to see their destiny. That's why they believe only in the obvious physical realities, which can be seen with the human eye. Your destiny is seen by an inner eye, which is mystic. Cynics don't know about mysticism. They're disabled in this arena. And they're dangerous, because they don't know that they're disabled. They think they're perfectly clear, but in fact, they're perfectly blind.

"We need people who dream of things that never were." This is the president of the United States saying that we need wizards, sorcerers, and mystics. We need imagination. We need ideas. We need people who are willing to stand in the face of all that's known, real, and given. And we need them to dream in the face of this overwhelming reality. This is the part of us that loves *The Wizard of Oz.* This is the wizard in us. This is what we're meant for. Do not feel childish for being drawn to wild dreams, even though the cynics will attempt to make you feel just that. It's your nature to be drawn to these things. You're normal!

All you need in order to be a cynic is a set of vocal chords. And whenever someone starts talking about a dream, cynicism starts showing up, like pigeons around bread scraps. In 1927, when movies were exclusively silent and the idea of putting sound in them was being proposed, Harry M. Warner, the head of Warner Brothers Studios, asked, "Who the hell would want to hear actors talk?" When my dad said he wanted to do the Montana AIDS Vaccine Ride with me, the voice of cynicism said, "He can't do that. Find something easier for him."

What are the things you "know" you could never achieve? What are the things you "know" we as a society could never achieve? What part does cynicism play in your life? Where does that come from? What do you remember you didn't do because you were told you couldn't? How do you feel about that?

Cynicism in History

The chairman and president of Federal Express Corporation, Frederick Smith, wrote a term paper in college about how he viewed the passenger route systems used by most air-freight shippers at the time as economically inadequate. In the paper, Smith apparently said that a system needed to be designed specifically for air freight that could accommodate time-sensitive shipments such as medicine, electronics, and urgent financial transfers. Saying that the idea wasn't feasible, his professor gave him a "C" on the paper. According to its 1998 annual report, FedEx made more than $16.7 billion in annual revenues.

Thomas Watson, the chairman of IBM in 1943, said, "I believe there is a world market for maybe five computers," and 34 years later, Ken Olsen, the president, chairman, and founder of Digital Equipment Corporation, followed right along and predicted, "There is no reason for any individual to have a computer in their home." It's easy to laugh at these people now. But consider that someday, people will laugh at the things you and I accept as facts today: Human beings have to eat. Oxygen is necessary for human life. Gravity necessarily pulls things toward the earth. The earth has room for, at most, 20 billion people. Has anyone ever considered how many people the earth could hold if we were all miniaturized?

That sounds ridiculous, you say. Well, dreams always sound ridiculous. That's the nature of a dream—if it doesn't sound a bit ridiculous, it's not a dream. Imagine Henry Ford. He has this idea for a car, which he wants to mass produce. He's sitting around a table at Christmastime with his uncle, and he says he has this idea. The only thing he needs to make it a reality is for the government to pay for the paving of six million miles of road with two separate layers of asphalt; the installation of seven million traffic lights and five million stop signs; and all the roads need to be painted with yellow stripes that reflect light at night. Does that not sound ridiculous?

How about Thomas Edison? He invents the lightbulb. Now, all he needs to make it work is for the government to run 50 million miles of wire along every street in every city and town in the country, preferably on wooden poles that stand 30 feet high, which have been soaked in creosote so they won't rot, and then run a wire encased in rubber from each pole to each of the 30 million houses in the United States. Sounds a little ridiculous, doesn't it?

In 1876, Western Union said, "This 'telephone' has too many short-comings to be seriously considered as a means of communication. The device is inherently of no value to us." In 1899, another genius, Charles Duell, commissioner of the U.S. Office of Patents, said, "Everything that can be invented has been invented." That's probably my favorite.

Robert Goddard was the father of modern rocketry. In 1921, the *New York Times* wrote: "Professor Goddard does not know the relation between action and reaction and the need to have something better than a vacuum against which to react. He seems to lack the basic knowledge ladled out daily in high schools." But his basic principle, that a rocket's thrust creates an equal and opposite reaction against itself—even in the vacuum of space—was the simple principle behind the entire space program.

An early investment analysis of the radio concluded, "The wireless music box has no imaginable commercial value. Who would pay for a message sent to nobody in particular?"

Arthur Schlesinger, a special assistant to President Kennedy, wrote on President Franklin Roosevelt: "FDR had buoyant faith in the readiness of Americans to try something new. He also recognized that if you want to change things, you must expect hostility from those who benefit from the status quo. 'Judge me,' he said, 'by the enemies I have made'—and he had plenty among the economic royalists of his day. FDR rallied the people to the cause of experiment."

FDR understood the reality of cynicism in the world, and he was prepared for it. When you're prepared for things like cynicism, then those things no longer surprise you. This part of the book is designed to help you anticipate the cynicism, and to help you avoid being surprised by comments and negativity that would otherwise derail you. That doesn't mean you can avoid cynicism—cynicism is a hard cold reality—it just means you can avoid being *surprised* by it.

If you had lived 100 years ago, do you think you would have believed we'd land a man on the moon? If you lived thousands of years ago, do you think you would have believed the earth was flat? What would you have thought of someone going around saying it was

round? What would you think today of someone who says they want to end world hunger in the next ten years? How has the voice of cynicism created disbelief in your own life?

Cynicism Inside Ourselves

So the real question is, who are these cynics, and how can you recognize them? I have bad news. *We're* the cynics, even though I've written this book and you're reading it. Cynicism is all around us and inside of us. Some people just lean toward it more than others. But the voice of cynicism lives inside of you as much as it does anyone else, and it's the cynic inside of you that's the one you need to be most on the lookout for—not just after your moment comes, but even while you're awaiting it.

Each of us has other personalities in our heads, and they constantly speak to us, during every waking hour of the day. To the degree that we think that what they're saying is the truth—we're not really aware of them.

You're not aware of the power these voices have in your life. And one of these voices—in fact, the loudest of them all—is the voice of cynicism. It's often a nasty, punishing voice. It's not at all loving, nurturing, caring, or supportive. It is not interested in you pursuing your dreams—it's fundamentally opposed to you pursuing your dreams. In fact, it's fundamentally opposed to change of any sort because it simply wants what is familiar and doesn't want what *isn't* familiar. It masks itself as you, or your "conscience," or your "gut"—it disguises itself as an important part of you so that you'll always listen to it.

One day I was speaking to a group of elementary school children in San Francisco. We were gathered in a church near the altar, and I sat on the floor with the kindergarten kids so we'd be on the same level. I told them about the little voice in our heads, and I asked them to be quiet for a minute and listen to the little voice. I was worried that they wouldn't get what I was talking about—which was my own little voice talking—that's how cunning it is. Anyway, one of the kids says, kind of shouting to his little friend next to him, "What's he talking about?" and I said, "That's it! That's it right there—the voice that just said that!" That's the little voice. It doesn't know it exists—and neither do you or I most of the time.

Learning to uncover the camouflage of the little voice on a consistent basis is an exercise that will serve your dreams very well.

What is your little voice saying right now? Did you know you had one? When do you listen to it?

If you close your eyes and allow yourself to be silent for a few minutes, you can get an awesome earful of all the things this voice, or the other voices, are telling you. You'll notice that there's a great background noise to your life that you were perhaps never even aware of before. And it's not quiet—it's a shouting match between all these competing voices all wanting your attention. Try this: First, just close your eyes and be silent. Time yourself and do it for about ten minutes. Forget about trying to hear any voices; just focus on listening to what "quiet" sounds like. Have you ever wondered or observed what that actually sounds like? You'll notice that it's not "quiet" at all. Again, forget about any voices or thoughts and just listen to what "quiet" sounds like. What you should notice is sort of a ringing sound in your ears.

Have you ever been to a noisy concert? If you have, then you know what I'm talking about. That ringing in your ears when you're trying to sleep after the concert is similar to what you're listening for in this exercise. It won't be nearly as loud as the ringing after a concert, but it will be there. Listen to it. Get to know it for about ten minutes. Let your ears go to the ringing—and let your eyes go to it, too. This is background noise. This ringing is there all the time, and you don't even notice it. It's covered over by all of the other sounds in your day. You're under the false impression that when it's quiet outside, it's quiet inside as well.

You may not want to try this exercise for ten minutes. Take note of just how much you don't want to try it for ten minutes. That will orient you to the power of the little voices. They don't want to be observed—they just want to chatter. I remember going to the Los Angeles Zen Center once for an Introduction to Meditation seminar. At first, they wanted us to meditate seated on a cushion for ten minutes. Ugh. I thought I would go bonkers. I had never really meditated before, and I'm a very fidgety person. After the ten-minute exercise, they took us into the little Zen chapel with all the veterans, all seated very piously in this beautiful, quiet, peaceful state. They told us to sit without moving for 30 minutes. It was the most hellish 30 minutes of my life—I wanted to run out of there screaming after 10. That's how intensely the little voices hate to be disturbed by consciousness.

Now, there's another level of background noise that's much louder and more distracting than the ringing. It controls your life, if you're unaware of it, and it keeps you from you dreams. It's the voice of cynicism, mixed in there with the chorus of other voices I just mentioned. You and I commonly refer to these voices as "thoughts." But if you really take a look at them, you'll notice that they're quite active and demanding. They have emotion. They have personality. They are much less innocuous than a "thought."

I'll give you an idea of what the voices are saying in my head right now so that you can get a sense of what I mean. Here we go: *Is this lame? Are people going to get any value out of what I'm saying? Who am I to be writing a book? You don't even meditate on a regular basis yourself these days—what the hell are you doing telling them to do it? I hope those loan documents get faxed over here. What's taking them so long? When is Jeff going to call with the directions for tonight?*

What else am I thinking to myself? *How many pages have I written? Four. How many pages should the book be? At least 200, I think. Once I have 200 pages then it will be a book. A book!? A book takes forever to write. I can't write a book.*

Look at how many of those thoughts were cynical. *Who am I to be writing a book? Is this lame? People won't really find this valuable.* Those voices are there all the time. And these things came up in just about 15 seconds. That's more than 17,000 cynical expressions running around your brain in a 24-hour period. They're there *all the time.* We try to live in the midst of all of this, and we wonder why we don't pursue our dreams. Who on earth could pursue their dreams in the face of all of this self-inflicted negativity? The voices of the cynics "out there" are only saying what the voices inside your own head have already told you. So, you can use them to help you. Tell a few people your dream and listen to how many reasons they come up with for why you can't make it come true. Then inventory your own voices to see if they aren't saying the exact same things—or, at the very least, agreeing with everything the cynics are telling you.

Yes, indeed, your moment will come, and as soon as it arrives, your cynicism will attempt to kill it. And cynicism is persistent. The only weapon you have against it—and it's a very powerful one—is your awareness. Consciousness is your weapon. It disarms cynicism completely.

This story was in a letter we received from one of our event participants. He talks about the voices in his own head that tried to stop him from doing something incredible:

"'Kubat, do it again!' 'It' was one of those inane physical fitness tests—the standing long jump to be exact. Why did I have to do it over? Did I inadvertently do something wrong? Did Coach Nelson miss my mark? Actually, the reason was this: of all the sophomore boys, I had the longest jump. Coach Nelson was sure it was a mistake. After all, how could someone who played in the orchestra, sang in the choir, and acted in plays accomplish such a feat? For more than 20 years, I allowed his doubt to keep me from pursuing anything physical. That was until 1996, when I rode a bicycle some 500 miles from Minneapolis to Chicago for the first time. While the Victory Ride for the other 1,446 riders came on the last day during closing ceremonies, mine came on the very first day. You see, as fate would have it, the first pit stop was at my old high school.

"I wondered what Coach Nelson would have thought and, ultimately, decided it really didn't matter. Participating in the first Twin Cities-Chicago AIDS Ride taught me not to accept limitations imposed by others. Nearly anything is possible if you work hard enough and believe in what you're doing. Prior to that first ride, my life seemed to be a never-ending succession of personal and professional setbacks. Nothing was powerful enough to break my downward spiral, until I saw the first newspaper ad for the Ride and attended an orientation session. The Ride gave me something positive to concentrate on, and yet, I had made commitments before and not followed through. Would I disappoint myself again and make matters worse? I was 50 pounds overweight and hadn't ridden a bicycle any distance in 16 years. Heck, I didn't even own a bike!

"Completing the Ride taught me the value of taking risks, setting goals and consistently working toward them. A profound sense of *accomplishment and optimism now fills me. The Ride continues to inspire me, so I continue to ride. Remember the turtle: He can't move forward unless he sticks his neck out!"*

— Gary Kubat

Here's another sentiment from a woman who did one of our rides:

"I'm 5'3" tall and weigh about 100 pounds. When I told people I was going to bike 500 miles, they sized me up and down, and then, with a face that stated clearly they thought I was out of my mind, they said 'YOU?!' The truth is, even though I knew nothing was going to stop me, I was also terrified that I wouldn't make it. Talk about mixed emotions! I would think, What if they're right? What if I can't make it? *Despite all the doubts and uncertainties, I did make it. I did not walk my bike one inch of that route. I did it! I'M POSSIBLE! And I'm doing it again next year!"*

— Nancy Bronk, Minneapolis, MN

When you really absorb the full impact that these cynical and demoralizing voices have had on your life, you may be overcome by a great sadness, because inside you is a creative, childlike spirit that wants to experiment and that wants to test its limits and explore its nature—but these voices are killing it. They've literally robbed you of your dreams. They've robbed you of your life. It's no laughing matter. It's incredibly tragic and sorrowful.

Your weapon against them is your awareness. Identify them for who they are. Pick a prayer, poem, or mantra and try to recite it for half an hour. Watch all the thoughts that try to interrupt you, and label them. Do this for several days. You'll begin to see them for what they really are. My telling you about it is not real. You have to experience it for yourself.

The reason that Gary let the voice of his coach manipulate him for so long was that he hadn't differentiated his coach's voice from his own. He thought his coach's sentiments were the truth, and that they were his sentiments, too. What did your high school coach or

gym teacher tell you that still stays with you? What about your parents? Whose voices are you still carrying around with you?

The Many Personalities of Cynicism

Cynicism will charge into you with a great veil of moral authority. I see the evidence of this in our own work at Pallotta TeamWorks. People typically have to raise $2,000 to $3,000 in order to participate in one of our events. Every once in a while, someone will come up to me and say, "This event discriminates against the poor, because they could never raise $2,500. You should set a lower fund-raising goal for the disenfranchised." So first of all, I'm being made to feel uncaring, heartless, and discriminatory. Yet the people who tell me this are typically unable to give me one instance in which they've ever done anything to help or empower the poor or disenfranchised in their entire lives. They've just developed this microwave moralism: All of a sudden—presto!—they're soldiers in the fight for social justice.

More important, they're attempting to kill off the idea that someone who's poor could actually accomplish the goal of raising $2,500. That flies in the face of everything they believe about the poor. It seems to me that one of the biggest things that keeps people stuck in poverty is the commonly held belief that they're small, incapable, and need our help. If we were to lower our pledge amount to $1,000 for someone who's poor, we would, in essence, be saying, "We're going to make this easier for you because we don't believe that you have the same capacity to accomplish this as people who are well off. You're *less* and they're *more*. You're small and they're big. You're $1,000 and they're $2,500. You don't belong in their league." Which is, of course, what people have been saying to the disadvantaged since the beginning of time.

It never dawns on a cynic to go out and help someone who's poor *raise* the money. It never dawns on a cynic to suggest a different alternative—like, maybe ask those who are affluent to raise more. But we do, in all of our events, encourage those who can afford it to raise more, and we've had people raise as much as $40,000, $60,000, and even—in the case of one woman from San Francisco—$100,000 for one event.

When we were doing the "Ride for Life," there were several occasions when people learned we were raising money to fight world hunger, and they actually said, "Why aren't you doing something about hunger in America?" I was so pissed. Inside, I'm thinking, *Why the hell aren't* you *doing something about hunger in America? Because we've already got our hands full riding across the goddamned entire United States on our bikes.* Here were people who weren't doing anything about hunger anywhere, and they felt so threatened by the magnitude of our dream that they had to try to put us in the morally inferior light of not caring about our own country. Cynicism is powerful and cunning stuff.

Whenever you're being made to feel bad, wrong, immoral, or selfish, you ought to get very suspicious. It may just be a sign that you're threatening people, or that you're threatening yourself with the scope of your vision. It may have absolutely nothing to do with the truth. You're being manipulated by someone's cynicism. Who are people to be judging you anyway? And who are you to be judging yourself and your dreams? Ask yourself, honestly, "What's really the truth?" It may very well be that the forces of cynicism are trying to wrestle your dream away from you.

Cynicism is cheap. It's always asking, "How much is this going to cost?" It's cheap—always supporting the cause of scarcity instead of a vision of bounty. It is always, therefore, afraid of spending any money: "That money should be going to help people who are starving instead of into some stupid rocket." But notice that the cynics were never crying for more money to be spent feeding the hungry *before* the dream of going to the moon came along. Moralistic, righteous rhetoric is one of cynicism's most cunning tools. If they can manipulate you into thinking you're a bad person for wanting to follow your dreams, then there's very little chance you'll proceed.

People get upset with us for spending $50,000 on an ad in the *New York Times* to recruit riders or walkers for one of our events. They think that money should go to charitable services. What they don't see is that it *is*. On the very first Boston-New York AIDSRide, Tanqueray gave us $40,000 to buy a full-page ad in the *New York Times*. That ad brought in 1,200 phone calls: about 400 of those people registered; about 300 of them rode and raised an average of over $2,000 each. So $600,000 was raised as a result of a $40,000 ad. But the cynics would have vetoed it.

Some of you may remember that there was a tragic fire on the launchpad during a test procedure for the Apollo 1 flight. During the test, the three astronauts that made up the crew were in the command module, with the hatch sealed. The cabin was pressurized with pure oxygen, and a spark subsequently created a fire. It took seven minutes for the hatch to open, and the crew died of asphyxiation in a horrible fire. Certain members of Congress began calling for an end to the moon mission. The congressional strategy was to demoralize the NASA people—to make them feel negligent, stupid, and almost criminal. Chances are, if you're pursuing a dream that's really visionary, you will, at some point, meet with the same intensity from some cynical force. Even the mother who wants to go back to school to become a teacher can face this from cynical voices that "moralize" her into thinking that what she is doing is wrong for her children.

Frank Borman, who would later command Apollo 8—the first mission to orbit the moon—was at those congressional hearings. He told Congress that this simply was "a failure of imagination"—a failure to imagine everything that could go wrong. Instead of blaming imagination for the tragedy, he took the stance that there wasn't *enough* imagination put into the project, and the congressional cynics didn't quite know how to respond to that. Instead of bowing his head and saying, "You're right, we have no business dreaming this big—it was foolish on our part and we'll stop," he refused to fall into the trap of being manipulated—he stood upon the strength of his convictions and his knowing, and said, essentially, "We need to get better at our dreaming."

There's an additional point here that's very interesting. During the Mercury, Gemini, and Apollo programs, there were several astronauts who died in their T-38 transport jets. These astronauts died in unfortunate and tragic, but rather ordinary, aviation accidents. No one ever raised a real concern. Why? It didn't threaten anyone. Flying a jet wasn't new, it wasn't dreamy, and it wouldn't upset the status quo. But the *moment* an astronaut died in the visionary, inventive Apollo command module—a symbol of the moon and beyond—the cynics went haywire. *Why aren't they going haywire over the 25 million people who will die of hunger and hunger-related disease this year?* Interesting question. *Why aren't they going haywire over the fact that 75 million adults and children will die of AIDS in the next 20 years if we don't find a vaccine? Why are they not up in arms?* There's a lot worth pondering in these thoughts.

Another face of cynicism is that it's always suspicious. After we exceeded our "impossible" goal on the very first California AIDSRide in 1993 by about $600,000, the cynics were right there, and they didn't skip a beat—"Yeah, but can you do it two years in a row? Don't you think you just used up everyone who was willing to do something like this?" They still do the same thing today—100,000 participants and $160 million later—they're asking me, "Yeah, but don't you think you're reaching the saturation point for this kind of thing?" Anyway, in 1995, California AIDSRide grossed an astonishing $5.5 million and became the most successful AIDS fund-raiser in history. The cynics still persisted: "Yeah, but look how much money—40 percent—is going into expenses"; "Yeah, but this will never last." Five years later, we grossed $11.1 million—an unheard-of sum for one fund-raiser like this. At that point, someone actually said to us, "Yes, but the Ride is getting too big." Their persistence and ingenuity is unbelievable.

Over the years, I've been criticized to death because we're a for-profit business helping charities. What's amazing is that our critics have never once attacked the for-profit businesses that are out there *hurting* charities. We've netted gigantic sums of money for AIDS and breast cancer, yet this is what I hear: "Yeah, but Dan Pallotta won't reveal his salary." "I've heard that Dan Pallotta makes $300,000 a year." Never once have I heard these people attack the $15- to $20-million salary packages of the people who make weapons or carcinogenic chemicals. Why is it okay to make a huge salary *damaging* the world but not okay to make a decent salary *helping* the world?

I've sat with reporters, as recently as a month ago, who wanted to interview me under the guise of their concern for charity. In a 60-minute interview, they spent 55 minutes talking about whether I make $250,000 or $300,000 a year, then they spent the remaining 5 minutes talking about the $160 million we've sent to charity, and the impact that's had on the suffering people of the world. Where does that tell you their real passion lies? They're passionate about their cynicism. Most of them never even want to talk to our charities—that's how little they actually care about the end result. They criticize us for being a for-profit business, when in fact, they work for the very for-profit institutions to which we pay huge dollars to advertise our charitable events.

Jonas Salk has found a cure for polio. "Yeah, but how long will it really last?" the cynics ask. A mother goes back to school and gets her degree. "Yeah, but what price did the kids have to pay?" The Pope apologizes for the Catholic Church's sins of the past. "Yeah, but there were several groups left out." Hands Across America actually got people to hold hands across the United States. "Yeah, but how much of the money actually went back to the homeless?"

Can you recall instances where you've achieved something extraordinary, or watched someone do something extraordinary, and observed the phenomenon I'm talking about? Have you ever experienced people being jealous of you, or frightened by your capacity for accomplishment?

This suspicion is designed to shrink you into a nonthreatening size. Richard Nixon created a new relationship for the United States and China. "Yes, but he was a criminal." Isn't it amazing how we support and adore our past presidents, but not our present ones? Look at the way Jimmy Carter was ridiculed when he was president, and scorned as a lightweight. Now, he's almost universally adored as one of the most intelligent, capable statesmen of our time. Why do you suppose that's true? Well it's because he's a lot less threatening now. Even Richard Nixon—look at how sorry everyone felt for him when he died, and how, in his later years, he was sought after for foreign policy advice and generally seen in a less harsh light than he was in August of 1974, when he was about to be impeached.

Cynicism also tries to frighten you. One of the most poignant examples of this for me was when I was learning to fly. I've wanted to fly ever since I was a kid. The day before I was supposed to do my first cross-country solo, which is around a 150-mile trip, I was overcome by thoughts that I would die. *I might die. I could die doing this.* Now, believe it or not, that's a healthy thought. It gives you the proper sense of respect for what you're doing. Oftentimes, fear is a very healthy emotion. If you had no fear of a hot stove, you'd be burning your hand every day. Fear has a genetic purpose.

But what followed my fear came straight from the mind of cynicism: "I might die, and I'd be smarter to quit right now. I should just quit. This is crazy. I don't want to die up there. I have a nice life—a great life. This is nuts—why would I want to risk it all for the sake of flying around up there in this tiny little plane?" Over the course of 24 hours, this fear really began to grip me. So I did some reflecting on it, and allowed myself to listen to all of the background noise. I just let it be. I didn't try to fight it—fighting the mind of cynicism is a no-win strategy. Fighting it might have sounded something like, "I will not die. I've been training my ass off. I've got a great instructor. I've been a great student. And there's no way I'm going to die." But instead, I just let it be. And I realized that the mind of cynicism was right—I might die.

So then, what were my options? They were: (1) to quit—to stay at home and live more safely, more practically, and let my dream go; or (2) do the best I could, be careful, study everything before the flight, and fly. Quit or fly? Quit or fly? The two options became metaphors for the way I wanted to live my life. I decided that I might very well die flying, but I would rather die in pursuit of my dreams than live with them buried forever. I'd rather die flying than live sleeping. So by allowing the mind of cynicism to be, and by letting its frightening message get through to me, I was also able to be enlightened.

When all else fails, cynicism ridicules you. Look at how many of the great dreams in the world were labeled "follies" by the cynics. Disneyland was called "Disney's Folly" before it actually opened. The riverboat was labeled someone's "folly." And it usually always revolved around some kind of invention—some new idea—someone's dream.

Evel Knievel wanted to fly across the Snake River Canyon in a rocket he and his team had built. He was laughed at.

"Above all, remember this—that anyone can laugh at an idea. Anyone can criticize a failure. Anyone can call you stupid. And when they do, who is the more fortunate being? The one laughing, or the one learning? We will live with the courage to be laughed at. History remembers courage. There are no monuments to critics."
— Pallotta TeamWorks creed

Cynicism is mean and biting. Again, this is because dreams advocate change—great dreams advocate great change, and great change incites great fear. So people add color to their "knowledge": "The wireless music box has *no imaginable* commercial value"; "The telephone is of *inherently no value*"; "*Who the hell* wants to hear actors talk?"

"Great spirits have always encountered violent opposition from mediocre minds. The mediocre mind is incapable of understanding the man who refuses to bow blindly to conventional prejudices and chooses instead to express his opinions courageously and honestly."
— Albert Einstein in the
New York Times, March 13, 1940
(from *The Quotable Einstein*, by Alice Calaprice)

Cynicism is cautious and slow. Cynics always point out the problems, which, we'll learn later, can work to your advantage. Cynicism is always wanting more plans, more investigation, more committees to study things before anyone moves forward. The idea is if you plan for it long enough, eventually you'll suck all of the momentum and excitement out of things and the dream will never come to fruition. Caution can be a very risky thing. Not wanting to take a risk can be the biggest risk of all. Not wanting to make *any* mistakes is a *huge* mistake.

At its darkest, cynicism is threatening, violent, and lethal. Witness Jesus, Martin Luther King, Jr., all those people hosed down in the streets of Selma, Malcolm X, Robert and John Kennedy, Nelson Mandela, the student standing in front of the tank in Tiananmen Square. Abraham Lincoln. Anwar Sadat. Gandhi. These people dreamed big dreams, and they were imprisoned, beaten, and killed for it. It's one thing if you want to build the world's greatest amusement park, but it's entirely another if you want to disprove the merits of cynicism with great, broad, sweeping endeavors, like world peace, justice for all, or an end to hunger and poverty. Huge, ominous forces will swell up around you. The mind of cynicism will gather up all of its resources to stop you.

Galileo was condemned in the late 17th century by the Roman Catholic Church for teaching that the earth revolves around the sun. In his book *Pale Blue Dot: A Vision of the Human Future in Space*, Carl Sagan recounted some of Galileo's and the Church's writings on the matter. In the Church's indictment of Galileo, they wrote, "The doctrine that the earth is neither the center of the universe nor immovable, but moves even with a daily rotation, is absurd, and both psychologically and theologically false, and at the least an error in faith."

Sagan describes "the Holy Inquisition ushering the elderly and infirm Galileo in to inspect the instruments of torture in the dungeons of the Church" in order to get him to reverse his teachings, which he did. Galileo wrote:

> *Having been admonished by the Holy Office entirely to abandon the false opinion that the Sun was the center of the universe and immovable, and that the Earth was not the center of the same and*

that it moves . . . I have been . . . suspected of heresy, that is, of having held and believed that the Sun is the center of the Universe and immovable, and that the Earth is not the center of the same, and that it does move . . . I abjure with a sincere heart and unfeigned faith, I curse and detest the same errors and heresies, and generally all and every error and sect contrary to the Holy Catholic Church.

How is the mind of cynicism diminishing you? Is it keeping you light years away from your dreams? You see, cynicism doesn't just lead you to put your dream off for a while. It convinces you to throw it away forever. It convinces you to abandon the pursuit of your destiny, wherein your dreams lie. It convinces you that it is utterly foolish, that you should never attempt it, and then it turns you against dreaming in principle. So, how is the mind of cynicism diminishing you? Is it keeping you light years away from your dreams? Does it convince you to abandon the pursuit of your destiny, wherein your dreams lie?

You have a dream. You have a calling. Yes, you do. You may have thrown it in the trash so long ago that you can't even remember it, or think you can't, but you once had a dream. I don't want you to try to force it, but I want you to keep the question about what it is alive. You have a calling, and you *can* make it come true. Even though your cynicism may tell you otherwise, you can make it come true.

"You can make it come true" is such a powerful statement that it immediately calls forth cynicism. The thought that ran through my head when I wrote this was, *These people have lives, families, kids to feed. What on earth are you doing telling them to go off and follow their dreams? You're going to ruin their lives and their families. You're going to raise people's hopes. Get them chasing after dreams they have no business chasing after. You're going to start fights between husbands and wives. People are going to get divorced. And all for what? To chase your big ideas about dreaming?* That's what was really there in my mind—that by telling you your dream can come true, I'm going to ruin your life. That's literally what the mind of cynicism says.

"Our deepest fear is not that we are inadequate. Our deepest fear is that we are powerful beyond measure. It is our light, not our darkness, that most frightens us. We ask ourselves, 'Who am I to be brilliant, gorgeous, talented, fabulous?' Actually, who are you not to be? You are a child of God. Your playing small doesn't serve the world. There's nothing enlightened about shrinking so that other people won't feel insecure around you. We are all meant to shine, as children do. We are born to make manifest the glory of God that is within us. It's not just in some of us. It's in everyone. As we let our own light shine, we unconsciously give other people permission to do the same. As we are liberated from our own fear, our presence automatically liberates others."

— Marianne Williamson

Cynicism has many faces. It's moralistic. It's cheap. It's suspicious. It frightens you. It's cautious and slow. It's mean. At its worst, it can be violent. Most important, it is inside of us. This cynicism—this doubt about ourselves—is the greatest enemy. We expect the enemy to come from the outside, in fact, it resides within.

Our Dreams Come Through the Filter of Cynicism

Your cynicism is going through the file cabinet of your dreams and ideas—deciding which ones it will hand to you and which ones it won't. Guess what? It's not handing you *any* of them. It's going into another file cabinet called "realistic goals," and it's handing you files from that one and telling you that *they're* your dreams. You're getting bad files.

As you start thinking about your calling and its dreams, you're saying no right off the bat to several of them because you know they can't come true. You're not even saying no. It's happening so fast that you don't even have any choice in the matter. Your cynicism is choosing. You're waiting to get to one that has a reasonable chance of coming true. The problem is, your definition of "reasonable" is created by your cynicism. It's infected you. You file past your deepest dreams onto the smaller and smaller ones, until you get to one that you know can come true. If you know it can come true, it isn't your dream. Dreams are things for which there is absolutely no evidence. Dreams are things that put you, by their very nature, into a new world—a world of mystery, where anything can happen. In a world where you know what will happen, only the things that you know will happen are allowed entry. You eliminate the mystery. You eliminate the unknown. But it's only in the world of the unknown that your dreams exist.

The nature of a dream is that it's impossible. That's okay. A dream ought to feel that it's virtually impossible for it to ever come true—as if there's no way. Why? Because your spirit is in search of the joy and the sense of living that comes from making impossible things possible. The only way to get to the joy of a dream come true is to follow a real dream. And real dreams never feel like they can come true. That's why it feels so beautiful beyond words when they *do* come true. You've delivered your-self, at that moment, into a new reality. And that's what your spirit is in search of—its true nature, its ability to make the impossible happen. If dreams always felt like they could come true, cynicism would be dead, and that wouldn't be any fun. Cynicism is part of the game. In many ways, it's the gatekeeper of dreaming.

The thought of a real dream coming true should send a shiver up your spine. Imagine no more hunger in the world, and no one dies of starvation—within the next five years. You go to Appalachia, and no one is hungry. You go to sub-Saharan Africa, and no one is hungry. You go to Bangladesh—no one is hungry. No more UNICEF. It's no longer needed. No more CARE. It's no longer needed. No photos of little chil-dren with huge bellies on death's doorstep. Everyone has enough to eat. More than enough to eat. It's impossible, and you and I *know* it. Not within five years. Maybe not within 100 years. Maybe not ever.

This is the way all dreams look before they happen. And, your dream being a dream, this is the way *your* dream looks. It looks so utter-ly overwhelmingly impossible that you don't even stop to consider it. This is the dread I talked about earlier. It doesn't "look" impossible. It doesn't "seem" impossible. It *is* impossible. And that's the beginning and the end of it—the mind of cynicism is that authoritative.

Cynicism Has a Lousy Track Record

The good news is that these voices are almost never right. They never have been. In fact, these voices are aware that you have the power to make your dreams happen. The cynics are quite aware that the dreamers will prevail if they are true to themselves. And so they yell louder and louder and meaner and meaner in the hope that they can keep you from ever even taking the first step down the path to your dream. Because they know that once you make that first step, they are beginning to lose you.

Look at the world around us, and see how many times the cynics have been wrong. The mind of cynicism has been wrong about virtually every major dream anyone has ever had and pursued. Look at the Empire State Building, and imagine the things the cynics said about it. Look at the telephone you will talk on sometime today. Look at the television you're going to watch tonight. Look at the country that you live in and the freedoms we enjoy. Look at the integration and the growing harmony between races in America. Look at the Washington Monument. Look at the interstate highway system.

Imagine the cavewoman trying to conceive of all of these things. Imagine a Pilgrim being told that a vehicle called a lunar module would be built, land on the moon, plant the flag of a great country that you are the seed of, and return to the earth in the exact spot on the ocean that was predicted. Then this thing called a helicopter would come, people with oxygen tanks would jump into the water, and the helicopter would pick the astronauts out of their space capsules and fly them to a metal ship 30 times longer than the Pilgrim's ship, with a gigantic road on top that these things called airplanes can land on.

Look at the fact that in 1992, the Roman Catholic Church repudiated its denunciation of Galileo.

Look at the lights that are illuminating your room right now, the book that you're reading—these are dreams, too. Look at the car you drive. The fax machine. The computer that you do your work on. The Internet. The Cassini probe that's hurtling out in space right now. These were dreams. Every single one of these things was a dream once.

In your wildest dreams, if you lived 300 years ago, you couldn't have imagined anything that has unfolded in our world. What are the things you can't imagine, because cynicism will not allow you to, 100 years from now? How about ten years from now? What are the dreams for your own life that cynicism is keeping you from? I'll tell you mine. I want to make a movie. I love movies. And ever since I was a kid, I used to pretend I was a director. But the cynicism in my own mind says, "If you want to make movies, you need to be on that career path from the time you're 18 years old. You're too old now." It minimizes me. It diminishes me. And it always seems to have the voice of authority. Because it says everything in non-negotiable sentences.

What evidence is there around you right now that dreams come true? What's near you right now that, one day, cynics would have laughed at as impossible? Were they right?

Looking Back at Those Impossible Dreams

Look at the way the future must have looked for some of the world's dreamers. Let's say there's no Disneyland. There's nothing remotely like Disneyland. It's 1945. People from New England don't fly to California for vacations. And this guy wants to build this $15 million amusement park with a robotic Abraham Lincoln, a Tomorrowland, a Fantasyland, and a Jungle Cruise. He wants it to have a futuristic electric monorail train that circles up above the park. He wants to build a replica of the Matterhorn Mountain and put a roller coaster inside of it, and then he wants it to go through water. He wants to have a steam railroad train that circumnavigates the whole park. But there aren't nearly enough people in California to make the thing a success. He needs people to come from all over America—and people don't fly all over the place, especially not to go to some "theme park."

Now let me ask you something. Does this seem a hell of a lot different from your own dream? Add in the fact that the company we're discussing here was four million dollars in debt to the bank already. So there was nowhere to get any money for this crazy place, and there was no way some banker was going to take a business plan seriously that calls for spending $15 million on something called a "theme park," 45 miles away from Los Angeles and 3,000 miles away from the entire East Coast. People will be expected to pay close to a whole day's salary to come in and look at a bunch of robots. And the plan calls for them to pay that price two or three days in a row to see the whole thing. Why, it would be just about as foolish as a bank considering the business plan for *your* dream.

Harrison Price, a consultant who helped Walt Disney find the site in Anaheim where Disneyland is now located, did an estimate that said that each park visitor would spend approximately three dollars (remember, Disneyland opened on July 17, 1955), and he predicted attendance of 2.5 to 3 million people each year. Instead, Disneyland, in its first year, drew four million customers, and they spent an average of five dollars each. In 1999, it cost adults $39 to get in, and children's tickets were $29. Last year, the parks had attendance of more than 70 million people—and that's not including EuroDisney. That figure is more than 20 times what Walt Disney's team envisioned in 1955.

Yes, your dream is foolish. You're as foolish and as crazy and as naive as Walt Disney. Imagine Martin Luther King, Jr., as he approached his calling, and the ideas that would make it manifest. Here he is, one man in his late 20s, in the largest industrial nation on earth, fed up with discrimination and prejudice. There was no political incorrectness then. African Americans were not featured in national ad campaigns. And some kid in his 20s is going to change that in less than ten years? No way. Challenge the entire white establishment of the largest industrial nation on earth and win? What do you suppose that dream looked like from inside of Martin Luther King's shoes?

What if we were to listen in on his own mind of cynicism? What was it telling him? *I'm too young. I'm only one person. I'm too big for my britches. We should take it slow. Not upset the establishment. Change takes time. Real civil rights will probably take 50 years or more. We shouldn't rush this. It's important to be practical. What about my family? Why drag them through all this? I have a nice life in a nice church. The more I think about it, the more crazy it seems. Free my people. Who the hell do I think I am? What if they don't want to be freed? Who's going to listen to me anyway?*

Can you appreciate the audacity that it takes to be in your 20s and actually believe that in ten years you could alter the course of a nation and the world? And, can you appreciate how impossible—not it "looks" or "feels" or "seems," but *is*—to do that standing in foresight, instead of hindsight? This is the way dreams look in foresight.

If these people had goals, and not dreams, guess where we'd be. We'd have an amusement park in California called Walt's Fun Arcade and it would have a merry-go-round and a little miniature train that went around a tiny mountain on a piece of plywood. Martin Luther King would have set his life toward the goal of eliminating discrimination in drinking fountains in the city of Atlanta, Georgia. John Kennedy would have said, "Someday we should go to the moon, but for now we need to improve commercial air travel." Can you imagine a world without the image of Neil Armstrong setting foot on the moon? Can you imagine a world with no Disneyland, DisneyWorld, Mickey Mouse, or Donald Duck? Can you imagine a world where your parents didn't accept their calling to be parents? Very sad. Well, that's what cynicism would take away from us. And that's what cynicism is taking away from you. It's vanquishing the world of your birthright—your imagination and your dreams. It's taking away your cure for polio, your four-minute mile. It's making your earth flat and unexplored. It's keeping your slavery intact. It's keeping you from flying. *The price for following your dreams isn't nearly as high as the price for following your cynicism.*

My own dream for Pallotta TeamWorks is that one day every American will have participated in one of our events, that our ideals will be household names, and that we'll fundamentally alter the way ordinary citizens impact the great causes of the world. I have to tell you that there are days when this feels utterly foolish, and I shy away from it. There are days when I don't tell people that this is my dream because I think they'll think I'm silly or that I'm an egomaniac. But those days are becoming fewer and farther between. Still, I'm susceptible to my own cynicism, and I always will be.

Think of some people whom you admire for their vision and their accomplishments? Can you imagine what the mind of cynicism was like for them? What would it have said?

Choose Your Dreams

When Steve Forbes suggested abolishing the entire IRS in his 1996 campaign, it sent a spark of excitement through all of us. But our collective mind said, *We can't do that. Can we? I don't think we can. I think there's some law written somewhere that says you can't make changes that big. Isn't there some law that says you can't have fun like that? That would be too much fun. Too exciting. Too much change all at once. I don't think we could take that. You start having a little fun like that and pretty soon people want to be having more fun. Next thing you know, people will want to start having fun all the time. And we can't do that. Abolish the IRS? No, I don't think we can do that.* And we wonder why things never seem to change. It takes so much effort to push something through the mind of cynicism that only the very courageous ever attempt it. You can *create* that courage in you.

We *could* abolish the IRS if we wanted to. Who's going to stop us? Our parents? Yes, our parents. Yes. Believe it or not, Mom and Dad. And that's where the mind of cynicism originated for us—in our relationship with our parents. Here we are, a nation of adults, afraid to abolish the IRS because we literally think that our parents would get mad at us. It was our parents who gave us our first no, our parents who gave us our first, "You can't do that." They got it from *their* parents, who got it from *their* parents.

So we live as adults on this beautiful blue planet acting as if it's not in our control to do with it what we want. We need to get our parents' permission first! Not only could we abolish the IRS if we wanted to, but we could start changing the lights in the traffic signals to blue, orange, and pink. We could change all the highway signs to red instead of green. We're adults. We don't need our parents' permission anymore. Why do the stripes in the road *have* to be yellow? We could make the minimum wage $15 an hour if we wanted to. We could create a four-day work week if we wanted to, and work harder on those four days than we ever do in five, because we'd be that more energized. We could move the capital of the nation around the country, so that every city got a shot at it once in a while: Boston for ten years, Seattle for ten years. We can do whatever we want, and we're pretending that that's not true.

I love this thing that Ralph Waldo Emerson said. It's one of the most revelatory things I've ever read:

> *Our age is retrospective. It builds the sepulchers of the fathers. It writes biographies, histories, and criticism. The foregoing generations beheld God and nature face to face; we, through their eyes. Why should not we also enjoy an original relation to the universe? Why should not we have the poetry and philosophy of insight and not of tradition, and a religion by revelation to us, and not the history of theirs? Why should we grope among the dry bones of the past, or put the living generation into masquerade out of its faded wardrobe? The sun shines today also. There are new lands, new men, new thought. Let us demand our own works and laws and worship.*
>
> — from Emerson's *Essays & Lectures*
> (© 1983 *Literary Classics of the United States*)

You're free to follow your dreams. You just need a ticket, which you can obtain by letting your moments come, by listening to your cynicism, and allowing it to be. Get a good earful of everything it's telling you, and everything the mind of cynicism in the outside world is telling you. Take it all in. Let it talk. And then when you've heard enough, choose. Choose to follow your dream.

To follow your dream is a tremendous act of self-regard. It's a matter of saying yes to your human nature—the nature that made you a child. It's also a matter of saying no to your cynicism. In the end, what it requires is courage. Ultimately, love requires courage. You have to be courageous enough to love yourself.

Chapter Six
The Awesome Power of Commitment

Susan's Story

This is a letter written from the hospital bed of a young woman—a fitness trainer—who had registered to do our 1996 Twin Cities-Chicago AIDSRide:

July 1996
Fellow Riders:

My name is Susan Silberman. I am a 28-year-old certified personal trainer from Chicago. I had been looking forward to participating in the Twin Cities-Chicago AIDSRide. Things, unfortunately, didn't go as I planned. On the morning of June 2nd, I left my house for a training ride. On the evening of June 4th, I awoke in unfamiliar surroundings.

I was to find out later that I was hit by a pickup at 9:30 a.m., driven by a drunk driver who had run a red light. My left femur was broken in three places, and had severed the main artery in my leg. My right foot was fractured and dislocated. It has been a grueling and painful four weeks in the hospital. I have had six surgeries, including the amputation of my left leg below the knee. During this period, I have had a great deal of time to reflect.

Just as I needed the help of concerned citizens, who didn't know me personally, so do the victims of AIDS. They're waiting for advancements that only your support and commitment to their cause can provide. I will not be riding with you today, but I will be with you in spirit. Hopefully, next year I will be able to cross the finish line. So, good luck to all of you. Thanks for allowing me this time. Have a safe journey.

Sincerely,
Susan Silberman, Rider #413

Shortly after Susan got out of the hospital, she committed to doing the 1997 Ride, not knowing how she would be able to, or if she would have a prosthetic that would make the journey possible. Susan completed the 1997 Twin Cities-Chicago AIDSRide, and made another commitment. She decided that in 1998 she would become a "Spokesbuster"—one of an elite group of heroes who do all five of the AIDSRides in one year—that's 27 days of riding 2,500 miles total, and a requirement to raise more than $10,000 in donations. She did it—she raised over $10,000, and rode the 2,500 miles to complete all five of the 1998 AIDSRides. Her courage was acknowledged on a nationwide scale when she was asked to tell her story on Oprah.

This chapter is about the power of commitment. *Without commitment, dreams don't come true.* To try to make a dream come true without commitment is like trying to drive without a car. It's not like trying to drive without a steering wheel. It's like trying to drive without a *car*. It's that absurd. Not only can you not drive without a car, the realm of driving itself doesn't even exist without one. Dreams come true in an arena, or a context, formed by a commitment. A dream can't come true without it. To use a different analogy, when you go skydiving, the second you step out of the plane, you've made a commitment.

If you don't step out, you can't skydive. At the same time, you must know that stepping out of that plane requires tremendous courage.

Most blame the circumstances of their lives for the failure of their dream, and for the absence of dreaming. Most people are sitting around waiting for the circumstances to fall into place, for everything to get to an easy place where it looks just right, and *then* they'll go for it. They want to reduce the likelihood of failure to zero. When the likelihood of failure gets close to zero, you're talking about reality, not dreams. Reality certainly isn't inspiring or enlivening.

I'm going to start with a quote that I keep around me always. I recommend that you read it several times. It was spoken by a man named W. H. Murray, who led the Scottish Himalayan Expedition:

> *Until one is committed, there is hesitancy—the chance to draw back—always ineffectiveness. Concerning all acts of initiative (and creation), there is one elementary truth, the ignorance of which kills countless ideas and splendid plans: that the moment one definitely commits oneself, then Providence moves, too. All sorts of things occur that would never otherwise have occurred. A whole stream of events issues from the decision, raising in one's favor all manner of unforeseen incidents and meetings and material assistance, which no man could have dreamed would have come his way. I have learned a deep respect for one of Goethe's couplets: "Whatever you can do, or dream you can do, begin it. Boldness has genius, power, and magic in it."*

Moving from "What If I Can't?" to "How Can I?"

"*Until one is committed, there is hesitancy.*" Have you ever noticed that in yourself? Before you're willing to commit yourself—when you're in that gray area between yes and no—there are questions, often nagging ones. There is doubt, confusion, and a wishy-washy feeling. It's not pretty. Sometimes people try to move forward without commitment, and then it's even less pretty. There's usually some kind of whining and general lack of courage that goes along with it.

Before there's a commitment, there are questions, and they're typically useless questions. "What if I can't?" kinds of questions don't really empower anything. After there's a commitment, the questions change. They become helpful tools toward reaching your dreams.

Let's say you want to leave your job and become a schoolteacher. Before you're committed, the questions sound like this: "What if I don't like it?" "What if I'm not smart enough to pass the accreditation program?" "What if I can't get into an accreditation program?" "What if I can't afford the extra classes I'll need to take?" These are largely useless questions.

The answer to almost all of the "what if" questions is simple: "This will be a failure." But instead of just coming right out and saying, "I'm afraid I'll fail"— which would actually be a very empowering thing to say because it would loosen that fear up and let it fall away—we ask these "what if" questions, which allow us to feign an inquiry into the matter when there's really no inquiry going on at all. An inquiry would be powerful: "What if I'm not smart enough to pass the accreditation program?" Then you don't get to be a teacher. "What if I can't get into an accreditation program?" Then you don't get to be a teacher. There's not an iota of mystery here. You see, there's no real inquiry going on here because the answers to all the questions aren't only obvious; they're all the same. That's not inquiry.

The "what if" questions are part of a state of hesitancy in which nothing truly powerful or remarkable can actually happen. They allow you to put off making any kind of a commitment, but under the guise that you're truly considering things.

There's this wonderful woman that I'll never forget named Sandra Guzman, who showed up at a registration meeting for California AIDSRide 2 in 1995. She's a little woman in size, and she had driven up to Los Angeles all the way from Tijuana—which is a good three-hour drive—to come to this meeting. She was already registered to do the Ride, so she was committed, but she forgot her commitment and was back in hesitancy. Commitment isn't something you make once; it's something you keep making. If you don't, you lose its power. That's why marriage is so powerful: It's a statement of commitment that has to be renewed every day. Otherwise, the dream fades away.

The Ride was only two weeks away. Each rider had to raise a minimum of $2,200 in order to participate. During the question-and-answer period for the meeting, Sandra stood up and said, "I've only raised $650. What if I can't raise the rest of the money?"

I said, "You'll raise the rest of the money—just don't think that way."

"Yes, but what if I don't?"

"You will."

"I know you think I will, but what if I don't?"

"You just have to stop thinking that way—you *will* raise the money."

This exchange went on and on. I was younger and not as wise, and didn't know better than to get into a positive-thinking game with someone who wasn't committed.

Finally, I said to Sandra, "If you don't raise the money, then you can't go—it's that simple." Ah—the truth. Amazing what the truth will do. It gave me clarity. Then I read her the W. H. Murray quote, and I told her that there's no power in being on the fence. You're just stuck in this "what if" land, which is a no-man's land, a dead end. I told her that instead of asking "What if I can't?" she should just commit herself, and then start asking, "How?" as in, "How am I going to raise the rest of the money?" That's a much more powerful and valuable question and leads to much more useful and instructive answers.

Have you ever been in Sandra's shoes? How did it feel? Did you feel like a powerful human being, or did you feel confused? Powerless? Why?

There's something I say at the end of every AIDSRide, Vaccine Ride, or Breast Cancer 3-Day registration meeting that I've led:

"There is one thing, and only one thing, that each and every person who's ever done one of our events, is doing one of our events, or ever will do one of our events has precisely, exactly, and completely in common. It's not that they're compassionate, although they are that. It's not that they're courageous, although they're that, too. What everyone and anyone who's ever done one of our events has in common precisely, exactly, and completely is that they

filled out the registration form. They chased down their demons and they moved beyond hesitancy and they declared: "Yes." And nothing is more difficult than that.

"The registration form is the golden ticket to all of the magic. It's the passport into the land of your dreams. It's the declaration of commitment. You could leave here tonight on the fence, all confused, or you could make a commitment, and actually leave here tonight as a registered rider in the California AIDSRide. The two options lead to very opposite feelings and results. If you commit and register, tonight will be a night you'll remember for years to come. It will be the night you registered for one of the greatest adventures of your life. You'll be all giddy, excited, a little afraid, and full of energy and ideas. You'll be calling your friends tomorrow to tell them what you just did. They'll be making donations to you. This could be a really great night for you. Or it could be a fairly average, or even less-than-average, evening full of hesitation—a reminder of every other time you hesitated in the face of a commitment that could have taken you to a magical place."

Commitment Needs a Date

People in the media have asked me, "When do you think we'll find a vaccine for AIDS?" Like the rest of us, they think that it's a question of science. I don't think it is—it's a question of commitment. We will find a vaccine by the date we've set in a commitment to finding a vaccine. The commitment will drive the science—science won't drive the commitment. The simple fact that we ask a question about a vaccine means that we see it. We have a vision of it. It's an idea whose time has come. But we must step out the door. We must commit to a date.

We need to know less about science and more about how great things get accomplished. In that way, we'll learn more about science.

Commitment occurs in a space-time continuum. This is very important. It doesn't occur in a *space* continuum. If you don't set a commitment in *time*, it's not a commitment, and this is what distinguishes a commitment from a wish or a want. When John Kennedy said in the early

'60s that we were going to go to the moon, he said we'd do it by the end of the decade. Neil Armstrong stepped foot on the moon on July 20, 1969. When Muhammad Ali said that he was going to beat George Foreman, he knew he was going to do it on January 18, 1971, and that he was going to have to be at the fight on that day at four in the morning, in the country of Zaire, in a stadium, in the boxing ring.

Everybody in the United States wishes we could cure multiple sclerosis. This is a *wish*, not a commitment. NASA is making plans for a trip to Mars. This is a *hope* for the future, not a commitment. There's no document with a date on it that says when we plan to land on Mars. There are no deadlines set in our nation or our world for curing cancer, ending poverty in Appalachia, cleaning the Colorado River, or traveling at the speed of light.

Deadlines in time inspire action and motivation. They cause us to do things that we might never have accomplished in 100 years. They raise the bar for our imagination, creativity, ingenuity, strength, stamina, energy level, productivity, efficiency, and everything else that's a factor in making things happen. So if a commitment doesn't incorporate *time* in some way, it's not really a commitment. It's a wish or a hope. Wishes and hopes can't make dreams come true—only a commitment can do that.

"ThinkAboutIt-itis"

One of the things I've noticed a lot of at our registration events is how often you hear people say, "I want to think about it." It's one of the gatekeepers to commitment. Commitment doesn't come from the head—it comes from the heart. I've noticed that my mind can cause a lot of problems when it comes to decisions of the heart. My moment comes, and then my head wants to get involved. Oftentimes it does, and it can thwart my moment. My head can end up causing me to put it off, or it can destroy my moment forever. As I said earlier, the fact that your moment has come guarantees absolutely nothing.

Often the need to "think about" things is really a euphemism for "I'm afraid," and because it's mislabeled, it gets in the way. If you could say,

"I'm afraid," you'd be able to break free of the fear, and actually get to the truth in your heart about your choice.

Contemplate all the things in your life that your heart really wanted to do, but that you said "I have to think about it" to. Did you ever actually dedicate any time afterward to thinking about it? Do you have a special chair or place or atmosphere you sit in to "think about" things? If not, how could you create it? After we've used that line to put off a commitment, most of us never think about things again.

"People in the West are always getting ready to live."
— Chinese proverb

Providence Moves

Let's look at the Murray quote again: *"Concerning all acts of initiative (and creation), there is one elementary truth, the ignorance of which kills countless ideas and splendid plans; that the moment one definitely commits oneself, then Providence moves, too. All sorts of things occur that would never otherwise have occurred. A whole stream of events issues from the decision, raising in one's favor all manner of unforeseen incidents and meetings and material assistance, which no man could have dreamed would have come his way."*

Sandra Guzman was a very courageous woman. What I didn't tell you earlier was that the reason she decided to do the Ride in the first place was to honor her brother, who had died of AIDS. So I asked her at the orientation, very seriously, to make a commitment to what was in her heart, and she agreed—very vulnerably, which is typically the context for most commitments. She said yes; she would do it. She didn't know *how*, but she would do it. Providence moved, and all sorts of things occurred that would never otherwise have happened. A whole stream of events issued from her commitment, which raised all manner of unforeseen incidents, meetings, and material assistance, which she could never have dreamed would have come her way. It was just like the quote says.

The moment Sandra said she would do it, I got inspired, which is exactly the affect a commitment has on those around you, and I asked her to repeat how much she had already raised. She said she had $650, against a $2,200 commitment. So she needed to raise $1,550 more. I said, right then and there, that I'd give her $250. Now, do you think I would have done that had she not made the commitment? People are inspired by dreamers. People want to invest in dreamers. They want a piece of that. And that's why I fell in love with Sandra Guzman, so to speak. After I said I'd give her $250, a couple in the back stood up and said that they'd planned to go on the Ride, but because of an injury, they were going to go along as volunteers instead. They were so inspired by her commitment that night that they told Sandra they'd like to partner with her to help with the rest of her fund-raising. All this great stuff started to happen that would never have happened without her commitment.

Cut to the California AIDSRide two weeks later: It was Day Three, and I was walking through our campsite in Santa Maria with some foam sleeping pads. Riders were coming in, and the place was beginning to get very busy. That Ride had about 1,800 riders and 400 crew, and that's a lot of people and bikes, especially when they're all swirling around one campsite. It was a very hot day. I heard a voice saying, "Dan, Dan, Dan . . ." I looked and saw this woman running toward me with a giant smile on her face. It's always hard to recognize people in their bike helmets, so she had to tell me that she was Sandra Guzman. She told me she had ended up raising $3,500 and was having the best time of her life.

This is a woman who will never again have to assume that she's incapable of something. It was a powerful learning experience for her. And the difference between what *did* happen and what *could have* happened is important. What did happen was joy, tears, people supporting one another, and a lot of money raised for AIDS. What could have happened was resignation, dejection, and a sense of weakness and hopelessness. Sandra's commitment made the difference and actually caused great things to start happening for her. The ignorance of this simple fact—that commitment catalyzes the world around you—kills people's dreams. It may very well be killing yours. Knowing this—the simple matter of just knowing that commitment has this power—can alter your entire perspective on your dreams, and on dreaming in general.

That "moment" when one commits is absolutely magical. You feel it in your bones. It inspires others to commit themselves as well.

Once again, I'm going to refer to the W. H. Murray quote: *"Whatever you can do, or dream you can do, begin it. Boldness has genius, power, and magic in it."* That's why we at Pallotta TeamWorks avoid focus groups when creating new initiatives. A focus group is a device used often in the advertising industry, where a marketing department will pull a bunch of ordinary citizens into a room, show them their new commercial or product, and ask, "Well, what do you think?" If the consumers say, "We like it," then the company launches the project. If the consumers don't like it, the company cans the project. This is why nothing very original happens in the world—because everything is tested to see if it fits within an existing sameness of mind.

Consultants always want us to focus group the AIDSRide or other new event concepts before we launch them in a new city. Let's look at what would have happened if we had done that back in 1993. There are nine million people in the greater Los Angeles area, and 878 of them registered for the very first AIDSRide. That's .0001 of the population—one person out of every 10,000 people. A focus group usually has about 50 people in it, and in all likelihood, each of those 50 people would have said no to our idea—as would the next 50, and the next 50, and so on. In fact, according to the laws of probability, if we focus-grouped 10,000 people, only one person would have said yes. We would have chucked the whole thing after the second group of 50 people because we weren't committed enough ourselves to believe we could inspire others to sign up.

A focus group necessarily connotes hesitation, and a lack of bravery and commitment. The question you go in asking people is: "Hey, look, we're *thinking* about doing this bike ride from San Francisco to Los Angeles, and we're *thinking* about asking people to raise $2,000 in order to go. Would you do it? Well, what if we made it only *four* days, because we're *thinking* about that, too? Would you do it then? What if we lowered the amount you had to raise to $1,000? Would you do it then?" It doesn't inspire anyone. There's no boldness, leadership, or commitment. People respond to leadership, and commitment is what inspires people to do something that they otherwise, in nine out of ten cases, would never do.

Imagine Martin Luther King, Jr., doing focus groups for his 1963 March on Washington: "Hey, look, we're *thinking* about doing this march on Washington. Would you come if it's about passing nondiscrimination laws in employment? If you think that's too much for blacks to be asking for, would you come if we just made it a solidarity march? Would that be more palatable?" I mean, it's sickening. "We're going. You wanna come?"— now *that* inspires people. That's what he did, and 200,000 people showed up. That's a risk. That's bold. That's brave. That makes people want to join. So that's what we did with the AIDSRide. We started running ads that said, "Hey, this thing is *happening*. There's a group of us who are determined, we think it's time, we think it's right, we know it won't be easy, but dammit, we're going to do this. We're riding for seven days from San Francisco to Los Angeles, 560 miles, and everyone who wants to come has to raise $2,000, no exceptions. You wanna come? Well, do you?"

What great dreams are you focus-grouping in your mind, wondering what people around you will think, or wondering if people will sign on?

If you don't make a commitment, then even in a focus group, people who would otherwise go if they saw someone was committed will say no, because there's nothing there to inspire them. When there's a commitment, providence moves. All kinds of things start to happen that just don't happen in the absence of any kind of a daring commitment. So make a commitment to something *without* knowing how it's going to turn out!

Commitment must necessarily be made in a state of uncertainty. Therein lies its power. We must be willing to step out of the plane, not knowing what it feels like to fall. This is what makes commitment inspiring.

I was watching a documentary on the BeeGees the other day, and I heard a remarkable thing. One of them said that when they were kids, they made a pact with each other that they would be famous one day. They had no evidence that it could happen, but they made that pact anyway. Pacts and commitments can take you to great places.

Take a look at this story about two brothers that appeared in the *Washington Post* in May of 1996:

Washington—On a hot Sunday in July, 1969, 5-year-old identical twins sitting on their living room floor and watching television shared a dream to touch the stars. At the moment Neil Armstrong took humankind's first step on the dusty moon, Mark and Scott Kelly decided they were going to be astronauts. Both of them. This week, NASA made it official. The 32-year-old identical twins from New Jersey, both fighter pilots at the Pautuxent River Naval Air Station in southern Maryland, were the first twins—and the first siblings—selected as astronauts in NASA's history.

More than 2,400 people applied to be astronauts this year. Of the 35 selected, 10 of them, including the Kelly brothers, were selected to be Shuttle pilots. "It's an honor," said Mark, who is six minutes older, ". . . to have the chance," his brother finished for him.

This is the kind of magic that results out of bold commitments, and this was a bold commitment. It wasn't just the whim of a pair of twins. They actually went out and did the things they would need to do to have a shot—they risked their futures, passed on all the other practical options they had, joined the Navy, and went to flight school. Basically, they gave up everything in pursuit of their dream. At the same time, when they made this commitment, they had no evidence that they could accomplish it.

The people who do our AIDSRides, 3-Days, and other events become skilled at setting goals and making commitments, and to me, this is what makes them inspiring. One of the quality standards at Pallotta TeamWorks is to "create inspiration." That can sound very difficult. How do you go out and create inspiration? Do you give motivational talks? No. Do you jump up and down and try to pump people up? No. It's simple, like most things in life—to create inspiration, you set examples. You make commitments—bold and brave ones—and keep them. And you follow through with them. This is how to create inspiration. Have you ever noticed that the people who go out on a limb and say they're going to do something that seems impossible make you want to be like them?

Commitment has a ripple effect. And it is powerful.

"I'm a small business owner in the oldest town in Ohio: Gnadenhutten, population 1,347. I was first invited to ride in the Boston–New York in 1997 as the stoker on my brother-in-law's tandem. He, three other friends, and I raised about $17,000 that first year. The following year, seven of us rode Twin Cities as Team Tusco and raised about $29,000. This past year, Team Tusco grew to 16 riders and one crew member, and we raised $50,000 for the D.C. Ride. For 2000, we're returning to the Twin Cities, have a goal of recruiting 25 riders, and raising at least $75,000. So far, we have 13–15 riders registered and many more considering it. We also expect to have Team Tusco offshoots riding Boston–New York, CA, DC (and Alaska!) totaling as many as 25 more riders.

"Having now raised more than $100,000 over the past few years, and starting with just a couple riders, we're reminded of the words of Margaret Mead: 'Never doubt that a small group of dedicated citizens can change the world. Indeed, it's the only thing that ever has.'"

— Mike Lauber, Rider #5399, AIDSRide Los Angeles

Commitment Is Different from a Wish

Commitment is different from a wish. It is different from a hope, or from what you want. You can want something until you're blue in the face, and it won't make one iota of difference in the world. Commitment, on the other hand, can change the course of nations and history, of families and relationships, and of lives. However, most people walk through life thinking that they're one and the same. I remember going to church as a kid, and at a certain point in the Mass, they would do the "Lord, Hear Our Prayer," as I called it. Now, I believe in prayer, and I pray regularly, but this part of the Mass typically went with the priest saying something like this: "For all of the poor people in the world, we pray to the Lord," and the congregation would respond, "Lord, hear our prayer."

"For the homeless people in our streets, we pray to the Lord."

Again, the congregation would say, "Lord, hear our prayer."

Even at the age of ten, this just struck me as a huge cop-out. Oh, sure, let God do all the work, as if God hasn't already given us everything we need in order to solve these problems. As if God is going to swoop down and take care of all the poor people without us having to lift a finger. As if we're helpless. Prayer without action is like hope without commitment.

This is what I was thinking about hope and commitment at the closing ceremonies for the 1997 California AIDSRide:

"Everybody's always wanting some sense of hope. Show me hope. I scoured every stretch of road you guys pedaled. I looked behind the trees. And I couldn't find any hope. Hope is a great big hoax. It's an illusion. I don't even know what it looks like. It's just some word made up by someone so they'd have something to sit around waiting for, instead of actually having to do anything.

"I didn't find any hope. But I'll tell you what I did find. I found $7.9 million in cold hard cash. And that's going to help a lot of people with AIDS. And that's real. And I can touch that. I found 2,300 people who aren't willing to sit around and do nothing, aren't willing to sit around and whine about why they can't do something—2,300 people who want to make a difference big time. And that's real. And I can see you.

"I also heard a crew supporting one another, people taking care of each other, and people talking about the future and their dreams for a change—and that's real. And I can hear that.

"But I didn't find any hope. And I don't really mind. Who needs hope? If you don't have any reason to feel hope, you can't have any reason to feel hopeless. We have each other. And maybe that's it—that's all there is.

"Look up in the sky. I don't see anyone. I don't see anything. Do you? I don't see some big spaceship with the word 'hope' printed on it coming down to solve all our problems. But look right next to you. That's what we've all been looking for. Each other. Because that's all we've got. We have to become the things we're hoping hope will bring us. Does that mean that there's no God? No. Who do you think gave us one another? Gave us everything we need to solve our problems?

"Hope isn't going to end the AIDS epidemic. A lot of people are going to die if we sit around waiting for hope to find a cure. The only thing that's going to end the AIDS epidemic is you and me. And I say we can end the AIDS epidemic in the next five years if we put our minds to it. And if Congress and the president want to be with us, welcome aboard. And if they can't see that big a vision, then we'll just have to show it to them. Because we don't need them to do it—we saw that this week. They weren't pitching the tents, pouring the water, and pedaling the bikes. We were.

"I just want to thank you all—not for giving me any sense of hope, but for giving me evidence. Evidence that there are at least 2,300 other people who feel the same. And that's all any of us needs to hold up a dream as big as ending AIDS. Thank you. People may say we are dreamers. Tell them to make no mistake. We are."

It's important to understand the distinction between hopes, wishes, wants, dreams—yes, even dreams—and commitment. Commitment is the thing that can make it happen—none of those other things can. A dream can't make a dream happen. A dream in the absence of a commitment is just a word. A dream *with* a commitment can change the world. If you don't understand the distinction, you'll go to your grave with all of your hopes, wishes, wants, and dreams unrealized. Because most of us think it's enough just to hope. People sit around in a job that they hate, and they dream all day long about where they really want to be. The dream carries them away and helps them forget about the drudgery of their day, and they think that's good. It's not good if it continues on without any commitment. The dream just becomes an escape from reality. It just ends up being a fantasy.

There's a great ad out right now for flying lessons that says, "Stop dreaming and start flying." This book isn't about daydreaming—it's about real dreaming—making your dreams come true. Dreaming, in and of itself, isn't ultimately satisfying. It's being in the game, pursuing the dream, overcoming the obstacles, making the commitment, and making it happen that is the ultimate source of joy and fulfillment.

John Kennedy was *committed* to the idea of going to the moon—he didn't wish it or hope it, he committed to it. And that's how we got there.

But notice what happens with other major issues where there is no commitment, only a wish. Take ending hunger, for instance. We're ineffective—none of the right questions get asked, none of the brilliant answers get revealed. Hunger persists. People die. Children starve.

When the colonists wanted independence, they committed to it. They declared it. The Declaration of Independence was so powerful—the commitment was so courageous—that it created the miracle called the United States of America. Do you realize that the United States was created by a person with an idea, who got other people involved? "We the People." That's the power of commitment. And that's the effectiveness that comes into being when a commitment like that is made.

Guess why we don't have a cure for cancer yet? There's no commitment. Sure, there's a lot of hard work, and tons of well-meaning and dedicated people working on the cause, but that does not mean that the basic laws of dreams don't apply. They do. As they say—no commitment, no effectiveness. I have no doubt that we will find a cure for cancer one day, but I also have no doubt that we could have found it 30 years earlier had we applied a commitment to it. A Declaration to End Cancer, signed by the president, ratified by the House and the Senate, signed by the governor of every state in the nation, and signed onto by every major research facility and medical school in the country. Can you imagine that? God, we're so much less courageous now, as the most powerful nation on earth, than that little clan of colonists was back in 1770. Bob Dylan said, "When you ain't got nothin', you ain't got nothin' to lose." It's true—the great enterprises of the world were founded by people who started out with nothing. But for the most part, the great enterprises of the world are now the most cautious. They've lost their ability to dream.

Imagine what the most powerful nation on earth could do if we exercised the same kind of courage and commitment that the colonists did. Or what if we had the same commitment George Washington had as he rowed across Valley Forge in the freezing cold with a group of men whose boots were full of holes and whose feet were frost-bitten, functioning only on the vapors of faith—with no idea of the contribution their commitment and their courage would make to the world. My God, there's almost nothing we couldn't do. The colonists risked everything. Imagine if the United States risked something big in *pursuit* of something big—the commitment would unleash a power that humanity has never known. World peace, the terraforming of Africa, a commitment to work to end poverty in ten nations in ten years, including our own—all of these things are possible.

Why would we have to stop at cancer? Why couldn't we have a Declaration to End Hunger by the year 2010, and a Declaration to End AIDS by 2005, fully backed and fully funded? There's no reason why. There's absolutely none, but for lack of commitment.

Does this commitment or lack of commitment have any bearing on the pursuit of your own dreams? Where are you lacking commitment with respect to a dream? How do you feel when you think about making a commitment?

Commitment Gives You a Context

Commitment creates the superstructure in which the making of the dream unfolds, in which all of the obstacles, triumphs, feelings, and everything else occurs. Without it, there's nothing to hold all of this; and with nothing to hold all of it, it all falls apart.

Werner Erhard wrote some brilliant stuff about context in his source document for the Hunger Project. The Hunger Project is about ending hunger in the world, and creating the political and popular will to do so. When it was founded, the goal was to end hunger by the year 2000. One of the things Erhard wrote about was how context generates content, or how having a context, which commitment creates, gets you thinking about things—planning, attacking obstacles, asking the right questions, and so on. Here he describes context as a building with respect to John Kennedy's goal of landing a man on the moon:

> The result of what Kennedy did can be understood by analogy. It is as if he created a building named "A man on the moon in ten years," and inside the building he put offices for all the various ideas, positions, notions, and people that had to do with space flight. The first office inside the front door of the building in 1961 [sic] would have been called "It can't be done." This office would have been inhabited by the skeptics and the cynics.

WHEN YOUR MOMENT COMES

A content or position is threatened by any opposite position. Given two opposing positions, only one can survive. On the other hand, a context gives space to, it literally allows, it even encourages, positions that are apparently the opposite. In fact, the most important position in a newly-created context is the position which appears to oppose the context.

This is sort of like what we will talk about in the next chapter—how obstacles, which appear to get in the way of your dreams, actually lead the way to them.

The Latin *contextus* means "a joining together, scheme, structure, equivalent to context(ere) to join by weaving." *Chambers 21st Century Dictionary* defines *context* as "the pieces of writing in a passage which surround a particular word, phrase, etc., and which contribute to the full meaning of the word, phrase, etc. in question." That's why they say that when you take something out of context, it doesn't make any sense.

Outside of a context, the obstacles lose their value. They no longer lead you to your dreams. In that setting, they really do stand in the way of your dreams. *Chambers* further defines *context* as "circumstances, background, or setting." Setting or background is a good analogy. The background noise in the context "A man on the moon in ten years," is "A man on the moon in ten years. A man on the moon in ten years. A man on the moon in ten years. A man on the moon in ten years."

It's like wallpaper. Now what happens if you throw "We don't have a lunar lander" into that background noise? It gets tossed in, turned over, churned around, ground out, and spit up into a solution called "Here's your lunar lander." What happens if you throw this into that background noise: "We can't"? It churns out "Why not?" And out of that come the answers. The context, generated by the commitment, does this.

Think of it as a giant fruit bowl, big enough to hold all of the doubts, fears, hopes, questions and answers. Inside a bowl like that, it's easier to see that the problems belong there. The doubts and fears belong there, too—every bit as much as the answers and the new ideas belong there. In that sense, since the problems are woven together with the solutions, they aren't as ominous or discouraging. They're more clearly seen as part of the process—they're integrated with everything else. They appear to be natural, as opposed to unnatural. But obstacles without context feel as if they don't belong. They feel unnatural. They create suffering instead of inquiry.

Right now, for example, it seems like I've been writing this book for months. I feel as if I'm never going to get this thing done, and maybe I don't even have that much to say. But I have a context to put it in called "a 200-page book in 100 days," and that helps to keep all that chatter from putting an end to the book. It also helps to improve the book. When someone says, "This isn't right," or "I don't like that chapter," it simply contributes to an inquiry that makes it a better chapter. Without the context, however, it becomes a reason to quit. Out of having a context, I know that complaints and despair belong in the fruit bowl, right alongside the exciting ideas and enthusiasm. You can't have one without the other. The context helps me put it all in perspective. Context is very powerful stuff—and commitment is what creates it.

There are a lot of people roaming around out there with a basketful of obstacles in their heads, with no context attached to any of them, and they create a general sense of despair in people's lives. "I can't leave the job because I've got a family to support. I can't get a new car right now—we don't have the money. I can't take piano lessons—I don't have the time what with the job and the kids and all." All this in one person's head! And this is just a very partial list! Imagine what kind of effect that has over a period of years—just listening to obstacles, over and over again, at every level, in the face of every new idea and every possibility, with nowhere to put any of them.

Commitments Are Created with Language

The sheer utterance of a commitment gives you energy. It immediately calls forth the process that would have to occur to make the dream happen. That's why New Year's resolutions feel so good—they inspire you with a new sense of you, and give you a glimpse at *I'mpossible*SM instead of *impossible*. Words can actually have a physical effect on us. If you've ever listened to a speech by Martin Luther King, Jr., you know that words can create a physical sensation. They have power—which brings us to how you create a context.

You create a context in commitment in language—in words. Language is the starting point for all of it. You don't need money, a team of consultants, or a business plan. You need courage. You need to take a risk. You need to make a commitment in the face of overwhelming odds. And you need to state it in words.

In a memo Walt Disney drafted in 1948 about Disneyland, you can see how it all begins with language—it all begins with saying so, and saying so can be a lot of fun:

> *The main village, which includes the Railroad Station, is built around a village green or informal park. In the park will be benches, a bandstand, drinking fountain, trees, and shrubs. It will be a place for people to sit and rest; mothers and grandmothers can watch over small children at play. I want it to be very relaxing, cool, and inviting.*
>
> *Around the park will be built the town. At one end will be the Railroad Station; at the other end, the Town Hall. The Hall will be built to represent a Town Hall, but actually we will use it as our administration building.*
>
> — from *Walt Disney: An American Original,* by Bob Thomas

Notice his language. "The Main Village *is* built around . . ." "In the park *will* be benches . . ." "Around the park *will* be built the town . . ." Notice how declarative the language is—he's literally bringing Disneyland into being with his words. Someone *said* the Eiffel Tower would be built. Someone *said* they were going to run a four-minute mile. Dreams can become reality *because you say so,* and we forget that. We think there's some kind of magic that has to happen. There isn't. It's about courage, risk-taking, determination, bravery, and then hard work. None of this is at odds with what we spoke about earlier—that is, the relaxed, spiritual process of allowing your dream to come to you. But once it has, it takes these other qualities to see it through. And the key to putting that all in motion is simple—it's your word. *Your word is the most powerful thing you have.* What you say, and, conversely, what you don't say, will have a great impact on your life. Think about that with respect to your own life.

Can you recall something that happened because you said so? Your marriage? A decision to have a child? A choice to leave a job and go back to school? Take an inventory of your life and look at all the examples you have of the power of your word—and the power of its absence.

This power that your word has must be wielded gracefully and compassionately. There's a dance you must orchestrate between the will of God and the tools She's given you, and you must be watchful not to mistake your own will for one of the tools that the universe has given you. You must exercise your word with humility. You must exercise your courage with humility. You must—all at once—not back away, yet not move forward solely of your own will. This takes practice, but it's important to me that you not take my advice here as a manifesto to charge forward with your life. It must be a graceful yet powerful act all at the same time.

Language has been the starting point for every great dream that you and I know. The AIDSRides got their beginning from some very powerful words I heard spoken in a movie in February of 1993. The movie was *Alive,* which is the story of a Uruguayan soccer team whose plane went down in the Andes. After three months, 30 of the survivors had died and there were only about 16 of them left. So 3 of the 16 decided that they had to try to climb out of the Andes and get to Chile if they were ever going to survive.

It was a ridiculous proposition—they had no equipment or winter clothing, and were wholly unprepared to make a journey like that—there were 10,000-foot snow-capped peaks everywhere, and Chile was nowhere in sight. It was truly impossible. At one particular low point, after they thought they had seen civilization but were mistaken, one of them says, "We're gonna die up here, man," and another says, "Well, if we're gonna die, we're gonna die walking." Those words spoke the commitment, and created the context. "We will walk until we get home or until we die, but we will not stop walking." Those were the words that moved me.

Eventually, they actually do make their way through the Andes and find Chile—and there's a spectacular scene at the end where the three return to the crash site. The remaining survivors hear the sounds of the helicopters, and they can't believe their eyes. They begin waving, cheering, and crying as the helicopters touch down to pick them up and bring them home, and in that moment you're struck to your very core by the magnificence and strength of the human spirit. It's a very *I'mpossible* sensation. It's a miracle—an awakening to the true majesty of what it means to be human. And you're saddened to think how many times you denied your own magnificence by listening to the negative voices in your head. That movie had a way of firing me up that few things have ever had in my life. I thought to myself that if these people could find their way out of the Andes, I could find a way to get over my doubts and put the AIDSRide together.

I walked out of the movie with my friend Ritch. I was stirred to my very soul, and I knew a moment was coming for me. I was very quiet and reflective. Without thinking about it, six words came from my gut, up my throat, into my mouth, onto my tongue, and rolled out into the world, without ever passing through my brain: "We're going to do the AIDSRide." That was it. The context was created. My moment had come.

There Will Come a Catalyst

I said that those words seemed to come up through my stomach without ever passing through my brain. Your job when your moment comes—when it really comes—is just to get out of the way and not block it. Your job is to *not* not allow it. It's a subtle act, this allowing, which is very, very different from forcing.

You have to relax and allow your dreams to come to you. Once they do, you have to step into action. But even here, there's a degree to which you have to allow it to keep coming to you—to cooperate with the will of the universe, instead of the will of your ego—especially in the weeks, days, and moments leading up to your plunge. You have to let it come to you, as opposed to pouncing on it. It's like trying to feed a seagull: If you move too quickly, you'll ruin the moment, and the seagull will fly away. Even though you may see the seagull, let it come to you. Relax. Be patient. Be inordinately patient. Seagulls don't come to people who are just patient. It can take hours—but the seagull will come.

Another way of saying this is that you do things when you're ready to do them, and you don't do things when you're not. That may seem to suggest that you don't have to act at all. It may sound like the opposite of what I've been saying so spiritedly here. It may sound like I'm saying that you don't have to make a commitment. That's not true—it's just that the action required is more graceful than what most of us are used to. A catalyst will arrive, and it's the last thing in the chain before you make the commitment. It's the immediate precursor, and it plays a critical role.

The conception of a dream occurs in a beautiful moment—it could probably be likened to conceiving a child through the act of making love. Conceiving a child is ideally the ultimate expression of loving another person. All the elements have to be just right: you're in love, you trust each other, you have a commitment to each other. But babies don't just happen—there has to be a catalyst. The circumstances have to be just right for this occasion: the timing, the feeling, the lighting, and the chemistry. You feel the moment coming on, you act—and out of that, a child is conceived.

Likewise, fulfilling a dream is a combination of elements. Everything has to be just so, and a variety of things has to converge in an instant. It's an art form, and it involves some letting go and some moving forward. That's the only way I can describe it. If you make it all about letting go, it won't happen, and if you make it all about pushing forward, it won't happen either. You simply cannot force this process. But rest assured, your catalyst *will* come.

Sandra Guzman wasn't ready to commit until I read her the quotation. My reading the quotation was a catalyst for her. The catalyst is the thing that occurs in the precise moment of choice. I don't know how to choose my dream in the absence of a catalyst. I need to know what my life is about, I need for my moment to come, and then I need a catalyst. *Alive* was a catalyst—I don't think the AIDSRides would have happened without it. The story I heard on the radio as I headed home from the beach so many summers ago was a catalyst—I don't think that "Ride for Life" would have happened without it.

I had the idea for the AIDSRides for a couple of years, but I seemed unable to act. Even after I got into therapy, I didn't feel moved to act. I was laying the groundwork so that when the catalyst fired, I would be moved, but I needed the catalyst. Don't force yourself to act before it's time. The catalyst will come, just as the dream will. Sometimes they will come together, at precisely the same moment—idea and catalyst will fly to you hand-in-hand. But sometimes the idea will come first, and you'll have to wait for the catalyst. That's okay. Be patient. But once the catalyst comes, don't you dare deny it. That's where you come in. That's your moment. Seize it. I could have left that movie, catalyst and all, and said no to the Rides. My role was to not say no. It was to say *no* to no. Don't worry so much about saying yes. Be ready to say no to no. God will present the yes. God will present the question. This may sound confusing, but you'll have to say no to no by allowing yes to come up from inside of you. Do you get it? Don't force the yes. Allow it. *The good news is that until the catalyst comes, there's nothing to do.*

In the end, this combination of idea, catalyst, and willingness, expressed in language, is how all of the great dreams we know became reality. It's a little-known fact that John Kennedy was catalyzed by a report Lyndon Johnson had brought to him that said NASA felt the moon landing was something we should do.

Can you identify a catalyst that led you to do something great in your life? Did you have to do anything in order for the catalyst to come? Did you have to do anything after it did?

We started out this chapter with a myth: that your dream will happen when all of the circumstances fall into place. It's a myth that keeps most people away from their dreams all their lives, because the circumstances almost never just fall into place. And we've explored the truth: that all of the circumstances *will* fall into place when you commit to your dream. We've explored the power of commitment, the need for context, and the power of language to maintain the context. We've now spoken about the arrival of a catalyst. Once you've made the commitment, the work in the physical universe begins—and that's the fun part.

Chapter Seven

Let the Obstacles Lead the Way

Some Observations about Barriers

"We can't go to the moon because the weight of the equipment required is too heavy for any of the rocket boosters we have." Obstacle. *"We can't go to the moon because we don't even have an idea about whether to land the whole ship, or build a separate ship that would taxi the astronauts there."* Obstacle. *"We can't go to the moon because we've never built a lunar taxi."* Obstacle. *"We can't go to the moon because we think the surface is powder and the ship will sink right into it like quicksand."* Obstacle. *"We can't go to the moon because we've never put a human being in space outside of a spacecraft."* Obstacle.

Obstacles seem to be between us and our dreams. You can have your dreams, so long as you get the obstacles out of the way. But in order to get your obstacles out of the way, you need to know what the obstacles are, and once you do, you'll see that they form the pathway to your dream. They are the stepping-stones. They are not blocks.

*"**Obstacle:** Something that stands in the way and obstructs progress; a hindrance, impediment, obstruction. Resistance, opposition, objection."*

— Oxford English Dictionary, 1999

Buckminster Fuller, the famous mathematician and philosopher, said that "a problem well stated is a problem well on its way to being solved." Most of us never get that far. We never take a good, thorough look at the problem. We get to the first obstacle, cynicism takes over, and we throw up our hands, admit defeat, and throw the obstacle (and our dream) in the trash. We don't *want* to look at obstacles, because they seem to spoil everything and because they aren't easy issues. And, of course, if an obstacle is a good reason to quit, then there are *always* plenty of good reasons to quit, because there are always going to be lots of obstacles, which makes giving up very convenient for us.

Here is a huge obstacle NASA faced in the '60s: "We can't go to the moon because the weight of the equipment required is too heavy for any of the rocket boosters we have." Let's break that down into well-stated problems. If we want to go to the moon, we're going to need a booster powerful enough to lift the equipment we need, right? Problem well stated and on its way to being solved. "We can't go to the moon because we don't even have an idea about whether we should land the whole ship, or build a separate ship that would taxi the astronauts there." Obstacle. If we want to go to the moon, we're going to have to know what vehicle should make the lunar landing—another problem well stated. "We can't go to the moon because we've never built a lunar taxi." Obstacle. So, if we're going to go to the moon, we're going to have to figure out how to build a lunar taxi. Another problem well stated. "We can't go to the moon because we think the surface is powder and the ship will sink." Obstacle. So, if we want to go to the moon, we're going to have to either figure out how to land in powder, or find a spot that isn't powder. Problem well stated.

One of the additional features of obstacles is that they layer themselves, and there are obstacles within obstacles. "We can't go to the moon because the weight of the equipment required is too heavy for any of the rocket boosters we have"—this is an obstacle. It leads to: "So, we need a bigger and better booster." Problem well stated. "But we can't build a better booster with the current kerosene and oxygen fuels we're using"—second-layer obstacle. This leads to: "So we'll have to come up with a better fuel combination." Problem well stated. "But we don't have the resources to tackle that problem and build a lunar module at the same time"—big obstacle, and the third layer. Leads to: "So we'll need more resources in order to do both." Problem well stated. "But the thing's going to have to be so huge, we have nowhere to build it"—another big obstacle in the fourth layer. This leads to: "So we'll have to build a building just to build the booster." Problem well stated.

This is a simplified version of that story. NASA needed a bigger booster rocket. So they went from the rockets that used to carry ballistic missiles to one completely designed from scratch for the purpose of going to the moon—the massive Saturn V. They changed the fuel to liquid nitrogen and oxygen—that handled the second obstacle. They hired a separate contractor, the Grumman Corporation, in Connecticut, to design and build the lunar module—that answered the third obstacle. They asked Congress for more money to pay for it—that took care of the next obstacle. They built a new building—the Vehicle Assembly Building—in order to put the Saturn V together. Another obstacle handled. Obstacles led to problems well stated, which led to solutions, which led directly to the surface of the moon.

You see, eventually, the list of well-stated obstacles becomes the blueprint for what you need in order to get the project completed. The obstacles have to be inventoried—the more exhaustive that process is, the more comprehensive the blueprint becomes. When you have blueprints, you can build things—when you have the blueprints of the obstacles, you can build your dreams.

I once read a statement by someone who said, "All my life I'd been trying to get rid of my problems. I'd been trying to get caught up so that there would be no more problems to deal with. Then, I knew my life could begin. Then one day it dawned on me: Life *is* the problems." In the same way, your dream is a configuration of problems that you solve, and that's actually why pursuing your dreams is an engaging and invigorating process. It's also why giving up is a de-energizing and depressing process—because trying to avoid problems is the same as trying to avoid life.

People think you have to know all of the answers before you get started. Not true. You have to know the questions. And the questions start with "How?" "How are we going to develop a great route for the AIDSRide?" "How can we build a stronger booster?" "How can we find out if the moon is made of powder?" "How can we build a bridge that will span the San Francisco Bay?" "How do I become an x-ray technician?" "How do I start the process of becoming a paramedic?"

Any great piece of architecture is a monument to the asking of proper questions. The Sears Tower, the Brooklyn Bridge, Saint Peter's Basillica, the United States Capitol building—there were millions of mathematical and engineering questions posed in order to create the blueprints for these buildings. Every structural obstacle had to be understood, overcome mathematically, and translated into drawings. Every problem had to be well stated. When you're in the planning stages of your dream, and when you're executing the solutions, time passes slowly—in fact, it disappears altogether. Why are we so scared of these obstacles? They're fun to work through. If you just sit down and start to "work the problem," so to speak—start to draw the blueprints—what's the worst thing that can happen?

Obstacles themselves aren't the obstacles to our dreams—our ignorance of the obstacles is the real obstruction.

Launching the AIDSRides

When we set about doing the very first AIDSRide, we began to develop a list of the problems we faced. It was a seven-day, 565-mile proposition. *Where are our riders going to sleep every night? We can't put them in hotels—that would be way too expensive. But if we don't have hotels, where are they going to take showers? Campgrounds? What if the campgrounds aren't where we need them to be? And can an average campground really provide showers for 500 people? What about food—how are we going to feed everyone? Are there any caterers that can feed that many people in one place, for one night, and then move their entire operation every day for six days? In the outdoors?*

What will they use for a kitchen?

What about the route? We don't have one—how are we going to develop a route? What about the inexperience of the riders? We're marketing this thing to people who've lost loved ones to AIDS, not to athletes. These people are compassionate, but they're not cyclists. What if they can't make it? What if they don't own bikes? What if someone gets hurt?

So this list of obstacles developed and grew. But we figured it all out, one obstacle at a time. We called local caterers—they said there was no way they could move their stuff night to night. We called mobile chemical toilet companies to see if anyone made a mobile shower—no such luck. So, we had no food and no showers. We were forced to become more resourceful, which is what really stubborn obstacles will do—they're actually the really fun ones.

We realized that there were other people out there who do multi-day bike rides—obstacles also require that you begin to reach out and ask for help. There was a bike ride in Oregon that crosses the state every year, and we knew that they used a company that has some kind of mobile shower and kitchen operation. I called this company and they said yes, they do have mobile shower units, and they can provide a mobile catering service. They were in business primarily to provide support to firefighters battling forest fires in remote areas.

It turns out it's not cheap to have rolling showers and kitchens. The cost was astronomical—big obstacle. But again, no obstacle is ever really an obstacle. It's just a catalyst for the right question. They needed a lot of money to drive all their trucks down to Los Angeles. The food and shower rentals were expensive. It had "no way" written all over it, but it really seemed like our only option. So what do you do when it looks like you can't afford something? Well, you need to examine the question. You need to state the problem better. You can't afford it given what assumptions? Well, one of our assumptions was that we needed to return a healthy percentage of the charitable dollars raised back to the cause, which was a good assumption. We couldn't have 100 percent of the fund-raising being eaten up by the expenses.

So ultimately, we decided that, in order to send much of the money back to the cause, people were just going to have to raise a heck of a lot more money than they're usually asked to raise for a charitable event.

How much more? *A lot.* The well-stated problem became, "People are going to have to raise $2,000 each." *Two thousand dollars?! Are you nuts?* my brain was telling me. *How are you going to get people who've never done anything like this before in their lives to ride their bikes 565 miles? And on top of it, you've got to get them to do something else they've never done in their lives—raise $2,000! You're crazy.* Obstacle. What's the solution to that? Well, if people don't know how to raise $2,000, we'll just have to teach them how to raise $2,000. We'll have to get them inspired about raising $2,000—which is what we did. The fact that something is difficult can actually be part of the appeal. It doesn't actually even have to be an obstacle. So we put together an elaborate set of tools, based on all of our knowledge of major gift fund-raising, and made it available to the participants. We also assigned each rider an on-staff coach—someone who would be there eight hours a day to encourage them, assist them, and offer advice and inspiration.

The result? The average rider raised $3,100. The top people raised $25,000—and some riders ended up bringing in more than *$40,000.* In total, we grossed $1.6 million—$600,000 more than we had budgeted—and were able to allow over 70 percent of the donations to remain for the cause.

There were lots of other obstacles, and they, too, led the way. We had no route, and no staff resources to develop a route. Well, why does staff have to develop the route? Why don't we get 20 of our most avid cyclists who've registered for the event already, and, instead of hiding the obstacle from them, tell them, "Hey—we don't have a route. How would you 20 like to be the ones who design the California AIDSRide route for all posterity?" Now that sounds exciting. We found those people, and they designed that route. A stunning route.

Within a few weeks of asking the initial questions, it became clear that we were going to need a number of committees to handle it all. So we formed a training committee, a route committee, a medical committee, a ceremonies committee, a public speaker's bureau, and a few others. In any given week, there might have been meetings for four or five of the committees going on—sometimes two different committee meetings going on in the same evening—all asking questions, stating problems, identifying obstacles, and cataloguing them. Then, once a month, all the committee chairs would come to my apartment for a dinner and group meeting to discuss the work of their committees. The more questions we answered, the more questions arose. There was a sense that it might all tip over. Sometimes, there were so many questions and issues that we had a sense the whole project was teetering—yet at the same time, we could feel progress being made. Every month, we could see how far we'd come from the previous month. There's nothing like doing something for the first time, nothing like discovering new obstacles and questions. To me, it's what life is all about.

Share and Befriend the Obstacles

Most of us are so full of insecurities that we never want to show any weakness. We never want people to know that a major piece of the puzzle is missing. We don't want them to know that we don't know something, and so, when a major obstacle presents itself, the sheer thought of keeping that a secret—which is what most of us do—is so overwhelming that we decide it's not worth it, and we quit.

This is the same for all of your dreams. Don't be afraid of the obstacles—befriend them. Don't run away from them; run toward them. Don't hide them; share them. Don't deny them; discover them. Look for them. Understand them—in detail. Think about an obstacle course. How do you get to the finish line? By following the obstacles, right? If you didn't have the obstacles to guide you, you'd never be able to find your way to the end of the course. The obstacle course teaches another important lesson: The obstacles are there for everyone to see. When you see footage of people trying to get through an obstacle course, it's usually done in groups. The whole group is trying to get through the course. There's a group support that develops—people start cheering for other people, and they start helping each other get over the wall. If the obstacles weren't there for everyone to see, no one would be helping anyone. But they're there, in plain view of the whole group. Nothing is hidden; therefore, no one can be in denial about any of the obstacles. That's the way it should be with your dreams. Start exposing the obstacles—start asking for help.

It takes courage to examine the obstacles. It takes a willingness to be vulnerable; a willingness to be laughed at—if not by others, then by your own cynicism. It's a sweet, childlike, innocent soul that has the courage to say, "I have a dream, and this is why I don't believe it can come true."

Are you willing to be that vulnerable? Are you willing to let down the guard of the "sensible one"? Are you willing to expose yourself to the cruelty of your own cynicism? Because that's the stuff that dreams are made of. That's the path that every dreamer before you has had to walk.

Questions Ignored

What are the questions we're ignoring for the future? What are the obstacles that we're not even aware of? I've often thought that leadership—real leadership—isn't about taking people places where they don't believe they can go. It's about taking people to places where they haven't even yet thought that they couldn't go. Places they haven't even imagined enough to believe that they can't get there. Places that *they don't know* they don't know about. The lack of a thorough understanding of the obstacles keeps those places out of reach. But the instant an obstacle appears, the dream necessarily appears with it. So unveiling the obstacles is the key to our dreams.

What are the obstacles—the key questions—that humanity isn't pursuing today? I believe that we ought to place our "How List" right next to the Constitution and the Declaration of Independence. We should have a national list of all the questions to which we seek answers so that we can begin to find the answers and check off some of the questions forever. *How could we end hunger in America? What would it take? How could we then end hunger in the world? How could we find a way to shelter everyone who is homeless?* You see, no one really walks around exploring these questions or the obstacles to their answers. The construct called "We cannot end hunger" is powerful in its invisibility. If we all began walking around next year bringing the obstacle to light, simply by saying, "We cannot end hunger.

We cannot end hunger. We cannot end hunger," the obstacle would gain some mass. Slowly, it would turn into "*Why* can't we end hunger?" then "*How* could we end hunger?" and then "These are the things we'd have to do to end hunger," and ultimately "These are the things we'll do *this year* to begin the process of ending hunger according to our plan."

All our lives we've looked negatively upon obstacles, but obstacles are wonderful things. They're life itself, the path to our growth. The universe won't remove obstacles—that's not part of what happens when your moment comes. When your moment comes, God unveils *all* of the obstacles. The question is, will you walk *toward* them, or *away* from them?

Chapter Eight

Dealing with the Desire to Quit

A Secret to Overcoming the Desire to Quit

The secret to overcoming the desire to quit when the going gets tough is to be committed to things that mean something important to you to begin with. It has to mean something to you to accomplish your dream, and it has to mean something to you if you quit. If it doesn't, why on earth would you want to continue? So don't make commitments to things you don't care about, deeply. If the things you're committed to are the things that your life is really about, you won't need any advice from me about dealing with the desire to quit.

After Alan finished studying for the grueling California bar exam, I bought him a bike—a SoftRide, it's called—it was a bike he'd had his eye on for a long time. I surprised him with it by putting it under the covers in bed with this note on top of it. For days afterward he kept saying, "I can't believe I have a SoftRide! I can't believe I have a SoftRide!" He loved that bike. He and I were going to do the Alaska AIDS Vaccine Ride together, and he was going to ride it. He never got to. After he died, I decided to do it myself on that SoftRide—wearing his helmet. Finishing that ride became very important to me. It was a way of memorializing Alan. It was part of what my life was about. And I wasn't about to quit.

This is the note I wrote to Alan when I gave him his bike:

> *Alan:*
>
> *This is to commemorate the enormous, inspiring amount of work you did to get yourself prepared for the bar exam, and to add the proper portion of fun and celebration to the fact that it's over. Flowers just wouldn't do. Every kid needs a new bike when the moment's as special as this. It's beautiful to me, the way, just over the last three days since you've been at the exam how much I miss you and how the sense of meaning, in the anticipation I feel about seeing you tonight, is special in a way that can only be explained by my increasing depth of feeling for you, and the more intimate knowledge I have of who you are with every passing day. You must make me one promise—that every time your little butt hits the seat of this bike, that you'll remember to ride safely, and that you'll always have a helmet on that cute little head of yours. I love you.*
>
> *Congratulations!*
> *Danny*

Most people quit. They get the desire to quit, they listen to it, and they run. Have you noticed that we're a society unable to sit with an urge? When we get an urge, we think we have to satisfy it. That's our total understanding of urges and impulses. Satisfy them. Act on them. We have no other approach to them. We react to impulses like a lion to a gazelle—get them and kill them. Feel hungry? Eat. Feel bored? Do something. Feel sad? Put on some happy music. Feel angry? Hit something, or yell. Feel a headache? Take an aspirin. Feel horny? Go have sex. Feel tired? Have a cup of coffee. Feel overwhelmed? Then by all means, quit. We haven't been trained to sit with our feelings.

What's it like to be hungry and to refrain from satisfying it? What's it like to experience being hungry? What's it like to feel sexual without acting on it? What's it like to want to have something and to go without? What's it like to want to quit and to refrain from quitting? Muhammad Ali once said, "I hated every minute of training. But I said to myself, suffer now, and live the rest of your life a champion." He refrained from quitting. What there was to experience in the absence of quitting was suffering, which he was willing to go through. Most of us aren't, so we indulge the urge to quit. It all stops there—no suffering. But what most of us forget is that when you do that, there's no championship either.

Chambers 21st Century Dictionary defines *entropy* as "the unavailability of energy for doing work," or "a measure of the amount of disorder in a system." *Oxford English Dictionary* defines it as "measure of the disorganization of the universe," or the "measure of a system's unavailability of thermal energy for conversion into mechanical energy." In my mind, it's the tendency toward spiraling downward. It's the physics of laziness. It's our tendency to always opt for that option that requires the least energy or effort. And the universe seems to be in a state of entropy. Spin a top, and after a while, it loses energy and sputters around, eventually falling down, eventually coming to permanent rest. Unless, that is, some force is brought to bear upon it to get it spinning, magnificently, again. That's the difference between the dullness of a top at rest and the magic of a top spinning—energy. A child can turn lifelessness into spinning magic by exerting energy, and that's what carrying on requires—energy. But giving up requires no energy whatsoever. Do you want to be a spinning top, or do you want to be lying on your side all the time, dormant?

Let's talk about feelings now. Once you've made a commitment, you have to start doing something. A commitment generates a process. You move out of the realm of things abstract and into the real world of frustration, anxiety, obstacles, pain, suffering, achievement, answers, people, personalities, red tape, money, no money, technology, arguments, breakdowns, and everything else. After you make a commitment, you begin to frame the problems. Then you have a blueprint, and you get working. Language creates commitment, which creates a context. A context then generates work, which generates achievement and failure. Achievement and failure then generate feelings. This is what we're going to talk about now. Feelings are the next roadblocks on the way to your dreams.

Judgments about Feelings

Part of the reason people quit is that they don't know how to act any other way. The desire to give up doesn't just pop up like a pager message in our brain and say, "I recommend that you quit now." If it were that simple, it would be easy. No, the desire to quit is like a drama queen. For those of you who haven't heard the term before, a drama queen is someone who can make burnt toast seem like the sinking of the Titanic—there's lots of hysteria, screaming, yelling, anxiety, stress, noise, and the like. The desire to quit is the same way. It never occurs insignificantly. It occurs as intense fear, danger, exhaustion, confusion, despair, depression, deep doubt, and judgment—and it puts on a hell of a show. So much so that you're no longer able to recognize it simply as the desire to quit—and that's how it gets you. Its disguises are masterful.

The first thing we typically do when we get the desire to quit is judge ourselves, and at that point, the game is over. The quitting has already won. When we get the desire to quit, it feels familiar to us, and we judge ourselves as being weak, wimpy, or unable to keep our word. We get a whole storm of negative thinking going on in our heads, and it gets so dramatic and windy in there that we no longer see that we have any choice in the matter.

This voice is nasty, punishing, mean, and relentless, and has been speaking to us all of our lives. It affects our lives in many more ways than just the ability to accomplish our dreams. It's a cruel voice. It's different from the mind of cynicism, which pretty much relegates its oversight to the arena of dreams. But *this* punishing voice takes free reign over most of your internal world. Its reach is much broader. It tells you that you're ugly. It tells you that you're fat. It looks at other people who are more successful than you and makes you feel that you're a piece of garbage—a real low-life, a weakling compared to them. It tells you that you're never going to be successful.

This voice tells you that you're not very smart; in fact, the voice says you're stupid. It tells you that you're lazy, that you don't work hard enough, aren't ambitious enough, and if you had any real brains, you'd be making a lot more money. It ultimately tells you that you're not good enough.

Today, let yourself be good enough.

The voice operates out of fear. It tells you that your world could all fall apart on any given day. It's a hypochondriac about its environment. It tells you that you could lose your job tomorrow, and then you and your family will be out on the street. It's always there, in the background, telling you that you *will* be homeless one day. You'll be disappointed. You'll come up short. It's the catalyst for all of the problems in the world. We're all running around so frightened of being homeless that we leave all of the homeless people behind. In turn, we see that we live in a world that leaves homeless people behind, so we run faster so we won't end up in their spot, which creates the vicious cycle of homelessness.

So when you get the urge to quit, this voice is right there. It pounces on you, and it's saying, "Of course you want to quit—you quit at everything. You should never have even attempted this in the first place. *You* can't make a dream come true. That's for other people, not you. Who do you think you are anyway? Loser. No book about dreaming is ever going to change that. You're no Walt Disney. Nelson Mandela? Ha! You want to compare yourself to Nelson Mandela? He's a whole other breed of person. You're not in his league. If you weren't a loser, you would have achieved something big a long time ago. You're getting too old now—give it up. Save a little bit of your dignity and just give up."

I know that all of this sounds harsh, but you and I both know that it's *not* an exaggeration. In fact, I'm probably being too mild. The overriding thrust of that voice is to tell you that you're basically a piece of crap.

If you take some serious time—over a period of months and years—to really examine this voice, you'll become filled from time to time with an incredible sadness. You'll see that *this voice*—not your boss or your neighbor—has been your worst enemy all of your life. No matter what you tried to do, it was never enough for it. It will always have a negative judgment of you.

Remember how we spoke about the mind of cynicism and how it pretends to have knowledge? In other words, you don't "think" you can't achieve your dreams, you "know" it? Cynicism has the effect of removing your ability to choose. It chooses for you, in a way. Well, the desire to quit does the same thing, and if you don't gain a lot of familiarity with it, it will take away your choice in the matter. In other words, you'll have no choice but to quit.

It makes sense to get to know this voice. The less you know it as a distinct entity, then, just like the voices of cynicism, the more you will confuse the voice with "you." Then when it wants to quit, you'll think "you" want to quit, and "you" *will*, for "its" sake, without even knowing it. Getting to know this voice is an act of kindness you make on behalf of yourself. Right now, you avoid this voice. When it comes to dreaming, you avoid it by quitting. As soon as it says "quit," you do. You never get to listen to its arguments, not at a conscious level, that is. But at a subconscious, semiconscious, and even unconscious level, you *are* listening to it, and it's making your life and your self-image miserable.

This is why I've never believed that positive thinking is a very smart thing with which to begin a process of real transformation. Positive thinking, to me, is avoidance thinking. It's denial. It's you trying to say, "I won't pay attention to the negative voices in my head, only the positive ones." If you don't pay attention to the negative voices, you never get in touch with the deep sadness that's there because of what they've said and done to you over the years. You gloss right over it as if it didn't exist. The sadness, believe it or not, will be the motivating force that eventually gives you the strength to lean toward the positive voices. But without the sadness, positive thinking is a short-term, short-lived gimmick, because there's no real motivating basis for changing your behavior. In fact, without knowledge of the negative voices, it's the negative voices that will get in there and convince you to abandon positive thinking. It's that insidious.

Sometimes you just need to get to the end of your rope, and you don't get there by positive thinking yourself to death. Sadness is a powerful motivator—it leads you to dream. Martin Luther King, Jr., was motivated by his deep anger and sadness over the treatment of his people. Beethoven wrote the Ninth Symphony ("Ode to Joy") in response to the sadness he felt over the child abuse he suffered at the hands of his father.

It pays you to get to know these voices—not to heed them, but to simply get to know them. What exactly is it that they say about you? What refrain have they been singing over and over again for as long as you can remember? What lies have they been telling you? Exactly how mean have they been to you? This is a process of examination that I recommend you begin now and continue for as long as you live, because the more you get to know these voices, the less power they will have over you—the more they'll lift—and you'll *honestly* feel your feelings—and the more you'll be able to truly dream and pursue your dreams.

These judgments come from voices inside you—voices that have been judging you all your life. So, now that you have a bit of awareness about the fact that they exist, what should you do with them when you hear them? In this case, it's more about what *not* to do when you hear them.

Actions in Reaction to Feelings

Here's an example that my friend Dick uses to shed light on the difference between commitment and feelings. Two people, let's call them Bob and Susan, are each planning to run a marathon and have begun training in the mornings. On the first morning, Bob's alarm clock rings at 5:30. He shuts it off, gets up, puts on his shorts, shirt, and jogging shoes, and goes out running. Susan's alarm clock also rings at 5:30. She turns it off, gets up, puts on her shorts, shirt, and jogging shoes, and goes out running.

On the second morning, Bob's alarm clock rings at 5:30 again. He looks at it, shuts it off, gets up, puts on his stuff, and goes out running. Susan's alarm clock also rings at 5:30. She looks at it, shuts it off, puts on her stuff, and goes for her run. All is well.

On the third day, Bob's alarm clock rings at 5:30. He looks at it, shuts it off, and gets up. It's raining. He says to himself, "I don't feel like running in the rain." He hops back into bed and returns to sleep. Susan's alarm clock rings at 5:30. She looks at it, shuts it off, and gets up. She sees that it's raining. She says to herself, "I don't feel like running in the rain." She puts on her shorts, shirt, shoes, and a jacket, and goes out for her run.

Here's the question: which person is acting out of their commitment, and which person is acting out of their feelings? The rain makes them both feel like quitting. The issue it highlights is that most people can't distinguish their *feelings* from their *commitments,* so when they get a "feeling," they act on it automatically, without thought or choice. It's as if they have no other option—they're that controlled by their feelings. But with practice, you can become directed by your commitments—by your word, instead of your feelings.

Feelings show up, like dreams, when they've a mind to. They don't care whether we want them there or not. When you get confused, you have your word to go back to. What was your commitment? If you're always guided by that commitment, and if what you're committed to is worth being committed to—if it really means something—at the level of your soul, it's much harder to be drawn astray by your feelings, no matter how intense they may be.

When I was riding in the Alaska Ride in the summer of 2000, on the second day, we had rain and very cold temperatures, and in the mountain passes, we actually had snow. I was on Alan's SoftRide, and I had a big commitment to this Ride. It was a 68-mile day. No sooner was I out of my tent than my feet and hands became wet because I didn't have waterproof gloves or shoe coverings. By mile 10, I was beginning to lose feeling in my feet and hands. I didn't feel well either. I was fighting off a cold.

By mile 15, at the first Outpost stop, things had gotten worse. I stopped briefly, and headed on up the hills toward Outpost Two. I wasn't going to quit. I just kept saying that to myself—"I'm not quitting." If I wasn't going to quit, then I needed a strategy for success, so my plan was simply to take it outpost to outpost. I decided not to think about the entire day, or about getting to camp, but to just focus on the current hour and on getting to the next outpost.

As I moved toward Outpost Two, I was trying everything to get feeling back into my hands and feet. I was swinging one arm while I held the handlebars with the other. Then I started kicking my feet out to try to force the blood down into the extremities. I tried sitting on my hands, one at a time. Nothing was really working. I made it to Outpost Two. Many people were dropping out, and when I saw that, the urge to quit got intense. It got very logical. But I decided I would press on. I put some plastic bags around my feet inside my shoes, and some surgical gloves over my hands.

The ride to Outpost Three was a grueling 20 miles, and this is where there was snow. Outpost Three was lunch. I knew if I could make it to lunch, I would have won the war of psychology. I'd be past the halfway point, and I felt that would motivate me to get to Outpost Four, and then on to camp.

The journey to Outpost Three was terrible. Every mile seemed like 20. The feeling was completely gone in my hands and feet, and I couldn't even feel my hands on the brakes. I was able to stop the bike, but I was unable to feel it happening. Every once in a while, other riders would pass me or I would pass them, and we'd offer each other brief words of encouragement. We were too absorbed in our own mental states to be much more giving than that. The numbness was making me want to quit. It was frightening me. I decided that if I was actually going to make it, I'd better deal with this fear. Ultimately, I decided that the numbness wasn't moving farther up my limbs, so I probably wasn't doing any permanent damage. I figured that, even though I wasn't used to it, I might as well just experience what it's like not to be able to feel my hands and feet. Once I let go of needing to feel them, that issue resolved itself, and I was able to keep the voices from nagging me about it.

Although I've been through experiences like this before, I found that the desire to quit was no less real or strong than it had ever been in my life. It was if I'd never encountered it before. It was as if I had to start from scratch, all over again, and I really hated that. I wanted to quit so bad.

I made it to Outpost Three. There was a warming building there— and lunch. I felt proud of myself for not giving in to the voices. I felt strong, and good about myself. That's always how it feels when I hold back the voices. I headed on the road from there, past gigantic walls of granite on the left; and dark, ominous, cold, wet skies on the right. The push to Outpost Four was difficult, but I had some feeling back in my hands and feet, as well as the satisfaction of some food in my stomach, and I was buoyed by the fact that this was the last Outpost before camp. I did make it to camp. I made it every mile. I had made a commitment that meant something to me, and I operated out of that commitment. I didn't quit. I wanted to quit. I felt like quitting every second, but I didn't.

Most people think that people who don't quit never want to quit. The opposite is true. *The people who don't quit always want to quit. They are haunted by that desire. They simply don't do it.*

Think about some times that you quit. Were you committed to something that was important to you, or was it important to someone else? What were the feelings that made you quit? In hindsight, how bad do you think it would have gotten if you hadn't quit? What did you miss out on because you quit? Can you see how your feelings took power over your word? How did they trick you? Did you have a context in which to put them? Did you know about context before now?

Fear Always Follows Commitment

Fear always follows commitment. The more you pursue dreams, the more you'll recognize this as a consistent pattern. It always, always happens. It's the nature of things. In my own case, there have been four clear examples of it in building Pallotta TeamWorks. The fear that followed the commitment was so intense and so real each time that the dream almost didn't make it.

The first time I experienced this myself was on Thanksgiving weekend in 1993. We were already four months into the organizing phase of our very first AIDSRide. A few other people and I headed up to San Francisco to actually bicycle four of the seven days of the route that had been scouted. We wanted to get a firsthand feel for it. The first day was about 95 miles—up some very steep inclines I hadn't trained for. By 4:30 or so, the sun was starting to go down, and my riding partner and I were only at about mile 60, and we were exhausted. We never completed the day.

The next day didn't go too much better. It was a horrific ordeal of pedaling that included this hill called the Vandenburg Grade that pretty much looks like what you might imagine a road directly to heaven would look like—except it's hell getting there. Again, we didn't complete the day. By this time my mind was in hysterics: *You have to call this whole thing off. It's way too difficult. And* you've *bicycled across America. Most of the people signing up for this event have never even ridden a single 85-mile day. They'll be dropping like flies. They will* all *want to quit.* We were committed—and then the fear followed. My own commitment was already backed up by the fact that 700 people were already signed up. That's when things got scary. When your mind senses that you're really going to do this, that's when the floodgates of fear and feelings open.

What I had forgotten was that it was natural for people to want to quit—that's what would make the experience heroic. My mind, on that Thanksgiving weekend, out of its own desire to quit, wanted to prevent any of the riders from ever having the feeling that they want to quit. If you don't ever feel like you want to quit, then you don't ever have a chance to figure out what you're going to do about it, so you can never really grow. You must have the feeling in order to confront it. If the feeling never comes up, then it means the experience was easy in the first place. I had forgotten that, and got caught up in the voices in my head. I didn't quit, and in May of 1994, 478 people did the ride—and none of them quit.

It's amazing how we underestimate people, and how we underestimate ourselves. We give no credit to the strength of the human spirit. We think that people will just up and quit at the drop of a hat because, in our own minds, the impulse to quit is that close to us. It's that close to everyone else, too. But human beings—some human beings—are truly miraculous. And it's because they're able to put that desire to quit in perspective—they're able to put it in context—that they go on and inspire the world. They keep pedaling. They persist. They move on, one step at a time, one day at a time, even while the voices are shouting at them. They carry the desire to quit with them—and press on.

The second incident was in the fall of 1994. We had completed the first California AIDSRide about five months earlier, and it was tremendously successful. So in early 1994, we started thinking about expanding the event to include a three-day ride from Boston to New York, which meant we would have to open an office in both cities. We went through four or five months of talks and negotiations with AIDS charities in both places, and finally, around August of 1994, we signed contracts with them and were slated to begin work.

Just a few days after the contract was signed, I was scheduled to take a red-eye flight to Boston. I started to panic. Thoughts started running through my head, like: *I have a nice little business in L.A. It's freezing cold half the year in Boston. No one's going to want to hear about a bike ride that's happening a year from now. And what are we going to do during all those winter months with a full staff running? No one will want to hear about an autumn bike ride in the dead of winter. No one will sign up. We'll go bankrupt. I have a great business—what do I want to go and screw it all up for by opening an office 3,000 miles away on the other end of the country? This will be the end of the company. This is really stupid.*

Then I started to think about *how* I could quit. *Well let's see, we've only spent $5,000 on the office lease so far, about $2,000 on T-shirts. Some money on the letterhead and stuff. So I'll lose $10,000. I think we can afford that. We'll just shut down the office right now and not spend another penny. I'll give the charity back the money they've put up, and we'll just stop it all right now before it goes any further, before any more money gets spent. It's the smart thing to do. It's cautious. It's prudent. I'll keep this nice little business I have, and we'll just keep doing the California AIDSRide and that will be it. That's it, just quit right now.*

I can't stress this enough: *If you don't act on feelings, they will pass. Feelings have a shelf life. They don't last forever—in fact, most feelings last about five minutes.* That intense desire to quit passes, too. None of us wants to sit with our feelings, so we rarely get to learn that feelings are temporary things. They go away. You don't have to *do* something about them to get them to go away—you just have to have the courage to sit with them for a while, and they'll go away on their very own. Try it. If you don't satisfy them, they'll pass.

For instance: Have you ever noticed that sometimes when you're really hungry, you get even hungrier while you're making a sandwich or waiting for the pizza to show up? While on the other hand, 20 minutes after you were starving, if you got sidetracked and didn't eat, the intensity of the feeling actually went away? Such is the transient nature of our feelings.

So I didn't quit. I didn't cancel the contract. People from Boston and New York signed up. They even signed up in the winter. We were supposed to gross $4.4 million—we actually grossed $7.4 million, and had I satisfied that momentary urge to quit, none of it would have ever happened. No $7.4 million. No 3,500 riders. No record broken. That's the price for quitting—you lose your dreams, and so does the world. And for what? So we won't be afraid for an extra 30 minutes while we ride the feelings out? That's quite a price to pay for something so temporary.

The third time this happened was in 1997, when we launched the first ever Breast Cancer 3-Day event. It was a three-day, 55-mile walk from Santa Barbara, California, all the way back to Malibu. Some time in November we were scheduled to run our first full-page, full-color ad in the main section of the Sunday *Los Angeles Times*. These ads cost about $45,000 at the time.

That's when the fear set in—right on schedule. *What are we doing here? We know bike rides, not walks. We know AIDS, not breast cancer. What if people don't want to walk for three days? Maybe people will think it's boring. What if nobody calls? Maybe this isn't such a good idea. The only reason the AIDSRides have been successful is because we market them to the gay community, which is very connected and chatty, and people tell their friends, who tell their friends, and things catch on. But there's no breast cancer community like that—this could be a disaster. We don't know the first thing about the audience we're marketing this to. We should stop it now before we run the first ad.*

Well, we didn't stop it. We ran the first ad, and it was the most successful newspaper ad we had ever run. We received more than 2,000 phone calls because of it. And the very first Breast Cancer 3-Day netted over four million dollars. Now we do them in nine cities around the United States, and in 2001 alone they will net about $50 million. We're doing 13 of them in 2002.

The fourth time this happened—and the most dramatically—was when we decided, in 1999, to launch Pallotta TeamWorks' Alaska AIDS Vaccine Ride. This was an entirely different proposition. Instead of the charities and the sponsors putting up the money to get things off the ground, this time I decided that we would go to a bank and get a loan ourselves, and that Pallotta TeamWorks would put up the money to get the thing off the ground. So we went to the bank and requested a $1.3 million line of credit to launch the event, and to introduce this brand-new way of doing things. We put together a very good presentation, and after a lot of follow-up and due diligence, the bank said yes.

We had done months of careful thinking about the event. We had a great marketing plan. We felt very confident about the need for something like this—the need to raise money specifically for vaccine research. But it was that yes from the bank that struck fear in my head. You know how they say, "Be careful what you ask for because you just might get it"? Well, it was that sort of feeling.

My mind started shifting into fifth gear. What was funny was that it was the exact same conversation as the one that had come up before the red-eye to Boston five years earlier: *This is ridiculous. I have a nice business. We have seven Breast Cancer 3-Days next year and five AIDSRides already. What on earth do you want to go and take on something as risky as this for? This is crazy. What if you're thinking that Alaska will be a great draw and it turns out people aren't interested in going there at all? What if people don't really care about a vaccine? Stop thinking so damned big all the time. It's grandiose. Quit while you're ahead. Just tell the bank you've decided against it. They might be a little miffed, but at least you'll avoid making this huge mistake.*

By this time I was sort of able to recognize the pattern, which helped—but it was still frightening. We didn't quit, of course. We took the loan, I signed the papers, and we ran the ads. We had hoped to register 1,800 riders in six months. In *two* months we registered 2,700 riders and had to close registration because we were oversold.

For the brochure for the event, we decided to write a preamble, just like the Constitution has. It says:

"We, the riders in the Alaska AIDS Vaccine Ride; in order to demonstrate to America the forgotten power of the ordinary citizen; in order to explore the explosive potential of a small group of human beings working with each other, instead of against each other; in order to remind all people of the world what Apollo 11 taught us— that we are capable of achieving the impossible, and that therein lies our joy, our legacy, and our reason for living; in order to incite an awakening from the sleep of resignation to the vitality of bravery

and commitment; in order to strengthen the fading resonance of the pioneering American spirit; in order to honor the memories and continue the legacies of every explorer, of the earth or of the heart, who ever stared down the impossible and showed the world a new reality; in order to bring an answer to the 300,000 HIV-infected Americans struggling to survive on protease inhibitors; in order to bring a vaccine to the 11 million people worldwide living in poverty with AIDS, for whom American miracle drugs are out of economic reach; in order to prevent the unnecessary death of millions of men, women, and children around the world who will be lost without a vaccine; in order to rejoin the visionary global compassion that defined the true meaning of America;

"Do hereby commit to travel to the ends of the earth together, with compassion in our hearts, and determination in our spirits, to undertake the first ever Alaska AIDS Vaccine Ride from Fairbanks to Anchorage, and bring the world closer to the eradication of AIDS by vaccine."

The preamble was our commitment. Naturally, it was followed by intense fear and a fierce desire to quit, just as you would now expect. I'm sure that this pattern will continue to repeat itself as we seek to undertake new event concepts, new ways of doing business, and new projects outside of the realm of comfort and the known.

By the way, the desire to quit follows a commitment in every realm of human endeavor, it's not just limited to business. Probably the most powerful place it shows up is in relationships. When a commitment gets made or a commitment is *close* to getting made, two people are faced with overcoming a hurdle that might really bring them close to one another or that might really create the intimacy they've always sought. Then, the desire to quit will come up so loud, frightening, real, and intense that it almost makes business matters pale in comparison. It's in that moment that the entire case you've been building in your mind *against* your partner will come up and start fighting like a litigator, urging you to dump the person. *They're too short anyway. Plus, I never really enjoyed the sex, and I'm feeling even less attracted now. This isn't the right person. I need someone who's more this or that. This person isn't this or that enough. This has been a nice person for now, but for the long haul, I really need someone who's a lot more this or that. I should just break up right now. I want my freedom back. I want to shop around. I need to see what else is out there.*

I remember when I was scared about the Alaska Ride, I started thinking that I should simplify my life, not enlarge it. What I meant was that I should make it more comfortable and less risky. Ever since I was a little kid, I've loved to build model rockets. I'd just purchased a kit for the biggest rocket I'd ever built—it was about three feet tall and used an entirely more powerful class of solid fuel engines than the ones I had built as a kid. I started thinking in my fear and despair that what I should do is sell the whole business—sell Pallotta TeamWorks. I should just go off to some small town somewhere, rent a space on Main Street, fix it up, and sell model rockets. I'd build them in the window, and kids would come in, ask about them, watch me build them, and it would be nice, cozy, and easy—with none of the stress, fear, and enormity of Pallotta TeamWorks. But then I had a thought: *What would I tell the kids? What would I tell them about rockets?* I would have to tell them to fly little model rockets but don't ever get involved in building a real one, because it's too stressful and risky, and it might fail. I'd have to say this, because that would be what I had done with my own life. It seemed antithetical to what rockets are all about to tell a kid to resign themselves to the miniature, pretend world of models, and never go out and try the real thing.

I had my answer. We're built to go out and try the real thing. That's why we're given imaginations. Funny, but model rockets are *based on* the real thing. The models didn't come first—they came after. Without anyone pursuing the great dreams, and realizing that rockets could fly, there would be no model rockets. Model rockets are aspiration objects.

So my advice to you is that you endeavor to understand the difference between your feelings and your word, your urges versus your commitments. Distinguish between the desire to quit and your heart's true desire. You'll always feel like quitting when you're pursuing a dream. The question is: What are you going to do about it?

Chapter Nine

Moments To Come

A Story about Timing

Remember how I said that the ideas come in their own time, and how Alan didn't arrive when I wanted him to, but when he did, he was right on time? Well, Alan didn't depart when I wanted him to either, but when he did, I guess he did it right on time. He left this earth when I was in the middle of writing this book, and the things I learned from him have made *When Your Moment Comes*, as well as my life, far richer than I could ever have dreamed. The universe has things in store for us more beautiful than anything we can imagine. If we're directed by our callings, allow things to come to us in their own time, and stick with them when they do, there's no telling what beauty and magnificence lie ahead. This is a letter that I wrote to Alan on the occasion of our six-month anniversary. I also read it at his funeral:

May 5, 1999

Dear Alan,

I'm sitting here at work and I'm thinking of you and what you mean to me. I really haven't known what to buy for you on this occasion as a gift. And I'm intimidated by whatever arts and crafts thingy you've been constructing in secret over the last week, so I haven't had any great creative, homemade ideas. I wish this anniversary fell a few weeks after your birthday. I'm fresh outta ideas! It's good that our real annual anniversary, which I look forward to sharing, will happen on the other end of the calendar from your birthday.

I know that material things and gestures aren't important to you, and that's one of the things I love about you. So, if I haven't picked up any flowers on the way to the restaurant, I don't have anything to give you but my thoughts and feelings. And here they are.

The reason I went into therapy, the reason I went into my twelve-step work, the reason I worked so hard to earn my maturity—every single therapy session, every tear, every page in my journal, every hour of meditation, every no I said to an unhealthy impulse, every prayer, every ounce of energy and effort I put into my spiritual and emotional path over the last eight years, was to create the space in my life for you to come in. I can't count the number of times I looked up at the stars over the years and wondered where you were and what you were doing. For the last two years, I've felt that I was in a monogamous relationship with you—I just hadn't met you yet. But I was sending good thoughts your way. Hoping that your nights weren't too lonely, that your Christmases were fun, that you were smiling and happy. That you had the same faith that I did that one day, our paths would converge, and the waiting would be over. Every time I looked in the empty chair across from me at the dinner table, I wondered when you'd show up. Sometimes my faith wavered, and I felt lonely and in despair. Sometimes I felt abandoned by God, and that love was something meant for others, but not for me. But not for long—I kept fighting that back.

And here you are: funnier than I imagined; more sensitive than I could ever have thought. More caring—I've never known caring like this outside of my parents—so how could I have imagined it? It's like imagining Disneyland when you've not been there yet. You make me feel like anything is possible. You confirm my basic instincts about the beauty of God and the universe—because I could never have imagined anything as sweet *and wonderful as you. My imagination was too limited. But I knew that it was—I knew that God had things in mind for me more beautiful than I could possibly imagine. And the funny thing is, it also means that God has things in mind for our path together more beautiful than I can imagine now.*

I love the mutuality of what we have together—the sense of parity, of partnership. The sense of shared values. I love knowing that you have the courage to walk into the unknown with me, and that, in fact, you want to. I love the courage you have to examine your past in therapy, I love that strength in you. I love that I can look deep into your eyes and you won't look away. I love that you love to talk about the good things and the difficult things.

I love the little kid in you, and I see more and more of him in those ridiculous little songs you write in your head, your handstands, your homemade candles, the bounce in your step when you get up in the morning. In fact, I think what I love the most about you is the little kid in you, because in him, I see the little kid in me. I see so much in you that is like me. You're so hard on yourself sometimes. You want everyone to be happy. You put a lot of pressure on yourself. You think a lot. A lot. And I know those things can cause pain, and can hurt the little kid inside. I know, because I do the same thing. And I feel that you, uniquely, because of all that, can understand me. And I've never been with anyone before that was so like me, that loving them was an act of loving myself as well. I've never been with anyone before with whom I felt I could be myself, in all my neuroses, and be understood, loved, and accepted for who I am just the way I am and just the way I am not. I feel that way with you.

I love the ways you're different from me. Your incredible concern for your friends. Your selflessness. Your sense of adventure. Your athletic ability. Your light-heartedness. Your love of books. Your ability to ask a perfect stranger on the beach to take our picture together. Your beautiful way with the written word. I love your letters and notes. You express things in such a rare and honest way. Your singing ability. Your beautiful blue eyes. The Civic. Your baking skills.

*Alan, the last six months with you have taught me more
about life, love, and myself than the 38 years before ever did.
I'm proud and happy to call you my boyfriend. And this day puts
a smile in my heart bigger than Mickey Mouse's. This morning I
was listening to some Disney music: "Zippity doo dah, zippity
ay—my oh my what a wonderful day," and "When you wish
upon a star, your dreams come true." And they both felt so
good, so right, and so true to my feelings today—six months
after the date I first met you. Thank God for Diana Dresser,
God's divine hand, and you, Alan John Gurd. Happy six months-
a-knowin'-me.*

Love,
Your Danny

*P.S. My dad always signs his notes to my mom, "Your Tony."
You're the first person I ever felt deserved that honor.*

I have many things that I envision on the path ahead. I have many visions
that frighten me, because they're so big. I don't know which ones will
come true or which ones I will pursue. I see a world at peace. I see people
being kind to one another—holding doors for others at the grocery store,
talking to one another, saying "hello" to perfect strangers. I see a person
with a flat tire, and I see seven, eight, nine, ten cars pulling over to help. I
see all of the people who pulled over to help talking to one another, like
they're all on one gigantic AIDSRide. I see presidential candidates running
for office with five great visions for their tenure: (1) End hunger in urban
Chicago as a test experiment; (2) send humans to Jupiter and return them
safely to the earth; (3) convert the entire country to solar-powered vehicles
within ten years; (4) adopt Botswana as a test nation for ending starvation
within ten years; and (5) create a "Manhattan Project" to cure cancer.

I see streets without litter. I see candidates such as Al Gore and
George W. Bush, when they see that the election is a tie, agreeing to serve
together to mend their personal differences, as well as the differences of

nations. I see a time when there are no more prisons, because children aren't raised in poverty and abuse. I see a time when alcoholism and drug addiction no longer exist, because people aren't raised in pain anymore. I see hovercraft on the highway, guided automatically without anyone needing to steer them. I see giant hotels in space, with beautiful views of the earth. I see a time without police, nuclear weapons, and armies. I see a time when we settle our differences with discourse, not guns, and we rise to the true potential for grace and civility that I believe is the promise of humanity. We aren't meant to be barbarians, carrying sticks and guns. We're meant to be the true dolphins of this planet, exploring the boundaries of our creativity gracefully, constantly pushing forward the definition of kindness.

I see an age when children go to museums to see what prisons and guns used to be, when they look at these artifacts under glass and laugh at what silly paranoias haunted their ancestors—the same way we laugh today at the people who thought Columbus would fall off the edge of the earth. I see a time when "crime" is removed from the dictionary, because it's a concept so foreign to our species as to have utterly lost any ability for people to comprehend. Other words will go with it. "Rape." "Murder." "Injustice." "Homophobia." "War."

I see a time when the notion that God is an 80-year-old Caucasian male with a long white beard and white robes who sends people to a place called hell—where a skinny little man in red leotards with a pitchfork burns human beings—is so utterly ridiculous that people feel only sorrow, not even ridicule, for the people who once believed these things—for the people once so driven by fear.

I see an end to people dying of AIDS and breast cancer. I see suicides coming to an end. I see great manifestations of spirit, where the metaphysical becomes as observable and legitimate as the physical. I see chocolate rivers and lollipop gardens. I see the countenance of a man who sees things manifest that are so beyond his wildest dreams, that his face at their sight alone makes me want to cry.

I also see smaller things. I see a new corporate headquarters for Pallotta TeamWorks—a giant place with trees inside of it, and tall 30-foot ceilings. Inside, people in the finance department hop on a bike to go 200 yards to the other end of the building to meet with the graphic designers about a new annual report for the years in which we just raised $400 million for charity. I see little electric trucks that drive around the place giving free ice cream to all the employees. I see huge scoreboards that light up and tell us how many registrants for our events we got this week. I see gigantic projection screens showing a different letter from one of our participants every hour, who are writing to us about the difference they're making in the world as a result of having participated in one of our events.

I see us imagining and producing more events that bring more and more Americans together to express their concern for the great problems that confront us. I see people walking to prevent suicide, bicycling to stop child abuse, swimming to end Alzheimer's disease. I see people marching across the United States for a great cause. I see people holding hands across the entire country in splendid expressions of unity. I see Republicans and Democrats walking together to end hunger. Actually, I've already seen *lots* of Republicans and Democrats walking, bicycling, and donating together to help great causes. I see multiple events converging on one another so that people who are walking to fight breast cancer cross paths with people who are bicycling to find a cure for childhood leukemia—and I see them all ending up in the same campsite that evening, where there are 10,000 or 20,000 people gathered in thousands and thousands of tents.

I also want to learn to fly helicopters, and I'd like to own one. I'd love to fly over our events and take pictures of our campsites. I'd love to produce great documentary movies that chronicle the kindnesses that occur inside the beautiful spirit of our events. I want to build a log home somewhere in the mountains, and ride horses on the plains below. I want to help people with great visions of impossible things get elected to the presidency. I want to fly in space and see the earth from afar. I would like to allow love to come again into my life, and watch it deepen and grow.

Much of this will be up to God. I'll have to see what moments seem to be coming. I have a great big toy box full of ideas. It's good to have ideas around, but I can't predict my future. I hope that in these pages I've steered you away from the idea of setting an aggressive, self-willed plan for manifesting your dreams. As I learned on the day that Alan died, nothing is guaranteed to us. I assume that I'll be alive when you read this book, but I have no assurance of that. I may die this evening, and that will have been the end of my mission. I may also live another 50 years, and perhaps my eyes will see many of the things I've mentioned above become reality.

My dreams to come are in God's hands. Yours are, too, I believe. Let's keep our eyes open for them. Let's continue to inquire as to what our lives are about, and allow our living to be the response to that question. Let's not *force* our futures and our dreams into being, but *allow* them. The world has had too much of forcing. The world needs more kindness— one person toward another, and each person toward themselves. This kindness can only be born of a detached approach, not a forced one.

I suppose when a person writes their first book, they ought to end it with some incredible words of their own. That supposition comes from those punishing voices of fear and ridicule. But I'll be kind to myself. I think it suffices to end this book with some incredible words that aren't my own—the ones that just happened to come to me in the moment. The words that come to mind right now are from Richard Bach, who wrote *Jonathan Livingston Seagull*. In his book *Illusions*, he wrote: *"Here is a test to find out if your mission in life is complete: If you're alive, it isn't."*

What is your life about?

ACKNOWLEDGMENTS

I would like to acknowledge everyone who helped me with this project.

Paiwei Wei, who said in September, 1999, "Hey, there are 100 days until the end of the millennium. It's a good time frame for a project." Alan, for his encouragement on the early drafts. Rex Wilder, for his constant enthusiasm. Chantal Westerman, for being a catalyst. Arielle Ford and Brian Hilliard, for being believers. Debbie Luican, for signing a book deal before there was a book. David Mixner, David Bohnett, Dr. David Ho, and Sheila Kuehl, for their thoughts on dreaming. Peter Anton, for telling me that I should tell people how I found *my* calling. Torie Osborne, Herb Hamsher, Steve Bennett, Dick Massimillian, Doreen Gonzalez, Neal Zevnick, and Maria Consineau, for all of their thoughtful input. Roger Housden, for extracting the first three chapters out of me. My mom and dad, for their encouragement on early drafts. Susan Silberman, Sandra Guzman, and all the little kids at the hospital for their inspiration. And to Sam Francis and all the others who wrote such kind praise for the cover.

I would like to acknowledge all the people at Pallotta TeamWorks who work so hard to make impossible dreams come true—the true believers—people such as Norm Bowling, Ed Neppl, Jeff Shuck, Robert Hartman, Carol Lane, Brian Pendleton, Curt Carlyle, Bryn Matthieu, Lisa Tabor, Mike Murphy, Alan Parker, Kenny Taylor, Jeff Masino, Joanne Buckley, Denny Chen for his help on the first draft of the cover, Laura Gilmore for all her help with clearances, Paul Warner, Andrew Fillipone, Janet O'Rourke, Patrick Jager, and all of our managing directors; everyone in our creative department; everyone in our administration, production, information technology, finance, and human resource departments; the unsung heroes in the Pledge Office, and all the crew coordinators, rider reps, ride guides, walker coaches, volunteer coordinators, and administrative folks out there in our field offices—people who believe when there is little to support the faith.

Thanks, too, to our business partners, especially Bob Petersen; and Ross, Howard, and Wade at OK's; Seth Perlman, Gail Krentzman, Mike

Bridge, and Chris, Howard, and Samantha at Bragman, Nyman, Cafarelli, and Regina, Patty, and all the folks at LaSalle who've been willing to believe in our untested dreams.

There are also the people who were with me in the early years of the company, when we were struggling to define ourselves, some of whom were true believers, and some of whom did their best—I thank all of you. I especially want to acknowledge Jeff Mallory, Sara Smith, Kevin Honeycutt, Michael Abels, Joel Safranek, Bill Barker, Lorri Jean, and the 1993 Board of Directors at the Center.

Thank you to all who have taught me, especially Irv Warner, the best fund-raiser in America.

I also want to acknowledge all of the people who have chosen the call to service—the good people who toil in the trenches of the poor, the sick, the dispossessed, and the disenfranchised—especially all those who work so tirelessly at the charitable organizations our events support—people at the San Francisco AIDS Foundation, The Los Angeles Gay and Lesbian Center, the Avon Breast Cancer Awareness Crusade, and all of the small community health organizations around the country they support. In addition, the UCLA AIDS Institute, the Emory Vaccine Center in Atlanta, the Aaron Diamond AIDS Research Center in New York, Food and Friends and the Whitman-Walker Clinic in Washington, D.C., the Callen-Lourde Health Center and the Lesbian and Gay Center in New York, the Fenway Community Health Center in Boston, and all the fine organizations that make up AIDS Events in Minnesota and AIDSCycle in Chicago. I want to acknowledge our new partners, too—the Liberty Hill Foundation, the American Foundation for Suicide Prevention, Vista del Mar, and Hollygrove.

I want to acknowledge the people who kept me safe and dreaming in my early years—my high school debate coach Freeman Frank, a modern-day saint; my sister Nancy, my partner in crime when we were toddlers and kids; her husband, Cecil; my sister, Susan, and her husband, David; my brother, Anthony; and my grandmother Hazel for not blinking an eye when they found out I was a little different—and for generally being great human beings. Chris, Jess, Hannah, and Max— thanks for being little dreamers. I also want to thank and acknowledge the Sunday Dinner Club—all my aunts and uncles and cousins who made childhood so rich; and the common, decent, everyday human beings who made childhood so colorful and taught me irreverence, from Joe D'Imeco to the Brunos and the Beaulieus and the Masses and the Prettis.

I want to acknowledge all the people in corporate America who have had the courage to believe in what were wholly untested ideas when we began—Larry Greifer and Peggy Bernstein at Tanqueray; Kathleen Walas and Andrea Jung at Avon; Joanne Mazurki and Pat Sterling; and all the folks at American Airlines, Clif Bar, UPS, Janus, I Martin, and the dozens of other small companies, hospitals, and bike and walking stores around the country that have been so generous with us and our participants.

I want to acknowledge the people who made Ride for Life a reality, especially Mark Takano and Michael Agliardo.

I want to remember all those who have died of AIDS and breast cancer, here and around the world, especially my friends, and the friends of my friends.

Finally, the friends who are living. Where would we be without friends? We wouldn't be dreaming, I know that. So many thanks to all of you who have and who continue to help me believe in myself every day— Randy Sturges, Ritch Esra, Bruce Dent, Clive Davis, Ignacio Valdes, Damon Wolfe, Michael Palumbo, Rosanna Giaccalone, David Alli, Steve Taminskis, Gavin Feinberg, Todd Warner, Loren Ostrow, Scott Hitt, Brian Niemark, Carla McNulty, Alex Wexler, Joe Argazzi, Rick Noll, Steven Gyllenhall, Jim Budman, Jeff Guthrie, Mark Rios, Phil Restaino, Judith Light, Robert Desiderio, Jonathan Stoller, Brian Newkirk, Jimmy Smith, Jeremy Bernard, David Wexler, Michael Arden, Steve Warren, George Herneghody, Lydia Vasias, Richard Soccarides and so many others.

And for anyone I've forgotten, forgive me. Know that you have my gratitude.

If You're Interested in Participating in a Pallotta TeamWorks Event

Every year, tens of thousands of people participate in a Pallotta TeamWorks event. They walk. They ride. They struggle together. They sing together. They see a new predictor of their own potential, and they see a new horizon for the world together.

If you're interested in receiving one of our catalogs, call 1-800-825-1000, or log-on to: **www.BeThePeople.com.**

When Your Moment Comes—The Practicum

For those of you who would like to explore the ideas in this book further, we offer a three-day practicum. It's more than a workshop, and it's completely different from a typical hotel conference room seminar. It moves. And it moves you. That means we'll actually be in the midst of people—our event heroes—who are practicing the principles we'll be talking about. This will be a whole lot more than a lot of theory. It's not for wimps. We won't be talking about goals and objectives. We'll be talking about dreams. We'll be talking about the things that make heroes *heroes*. We'll be asking you to confront those things that keep you from being the hero of your own life, and we'll ask you to move to a place where you inspire yourself to be that kind of person. We will ask you to leave with powerful commitments.

Our covenant with you is that you will leave the practicum less mystified about your own calling, and less mystified about what it would take for you to manifest your destiny. Each practicum happens on-site at one of our charitable events, but you will not be a participant in the event. Rather, the event will serve as a laboratory, one we will walk in and out of over the course of the three days in order to more fully explore what we're talking about during our facilitated sessions together. For instance, we'll spend part of one of our days on what to do when you feel like quitting. Then we'll go out to the top of one of the steepest grades on the participant route and find out specifically what kept the riders going all the way to the top. It all takes place in a multimedia big-top tent, which moves down the road at the end of the day. For more information, call 1-800-825-1000, or log-on to: **www.BeThePeople.com.**

Pallotta TeamWorks
2709 Media Center Drive, Building 1
Los Angeles, CA 90065

ABOUT THE AUTHOR

Dan Pallotta is chairman and chief executive officer of Pallotta TeamWorks, America's premier producer of human potential events, and the largest private-event fund-raising firm in the nation. He is a 1983 graduate of Harvard University. From one simple idea he had in 1994, his company has raised more money, more quickly, for the causes of AIDS and breast cancer than any known private-event operation in United States history—more than $160 million to date. In addition, these events have changed the lives of many of the more than 100,000 people who have been a part of them.

The vision of Pallotta TeamWorks is to change the world—first, by helping people to see beyond the limits they have for themselves; second, by helping them see beyond the limits they have placed on the world; and third, by spreading the simple power of human kindness. In addition to dreaming Pallotta TeamWorks' future, Dan is the volunteer chair of the AIDS Eradication Project of the UCLA AIDS Institute. He also volunteers his time working with hospitalized children.

Other Jodere Group Titles

Books

CROSSING OVER: The Stories Behind the Stories,
by John Edward

THE GAME: Win Your Life in 90 Days,
by Sarano Kelley

WHAT IF GOD WERE THE SUN?
a novel by John Edward

WHEN IN DOUBT, CHECK HIM OUT:
A Woman's Survival Guide,
by Joseph Culligan, Licensed Private Investigator

YOU CAN FIND ANYBODY!
by Joseph Culligan, Licensed Private Investigator

Audio Programs

CROSSING OVER: The Stories Behind the Stories,
an abridged audio book by John Edward

THE DARK SIDE OF THE LIGHT CHASERS:
Reclaiming Your Power, Creativity, Brilliance, and Dreams,
an abridged audio book by Debbie Ford

THE GAME: Win Your Life in 90 Days,
an abridged audio book by Sarano Kelley

HEAVEN ON EARTH: A Meditation with the Angels,
by Gary Quinn (both in audiocassette and CD)

WHAT IF GOD WERE THE SUN?
an unabridged audio book by John Edward

All of the above are available at your local bookstore,
by calling **Jodere Group, Inc.,** at **(800) 569-1002.**